CORE WORDS
For Classroom and Home

Developing Verbal Communication Skills and Augmentative and Alternative Communication (AAC) Abilities

A Practical Guide for Parents, Teachers, and Speech-Language Pathologists

JENNIFER JACOBS, MA, CCC-SLP

BLUE LAKE
PUBLISHING

Published by:
Blue Lake Publishing
Spring Lake, MI 49456
Bluelakecommunications.com

Crescendo 7x11 home in Proloquo2Go: ©2017 AssistiveWare.
For more information check out Assistiveware.com

Words for Life 84 One Hit: ©2018 Prentke Romich Company.
For more information check out aaclanguagelab.com

American Sign Language (ASL) signs pictured in this book
are referenced from William Vicar's Lifeprint.com

ISBN: 978-0-692-17337-4

*This book is dedicated
to my parents and sisters*

Positive Deviance

*The idea of building on capabilities people already have
rather than telling them how they have to change.*

—ATUL GAWANDE, FROM THE BOOK *BETTER*

The capabilities are there...we just need to know how to tap into them.

Contents

Preface vii

A Note to Families, Educators, and Speech-Language Pathologists 1

Core Words. 3

AAC—Augmentative and Alternative Communication 5

Reasons to Use AAC 7

Use of Routines to Communicate 9

Things to Keep in Mind 11

Use of a Prompt Hierarchy. 13

The Core Word Program 15

Core Word Weekly Outline 17

Core Word Guide

    Core Word Guide: "Do". 20

    Core Word Guide: "Finished, All Done" 22

    Core Word Guide: "Get" 24

    Core Word Guide: "Go". 26

    Core Word Guide: "Have" 28

    Core Word Guide: "He & She" 30

    Core Word Guide: "Help" 32

    Core Word Guide: "I". 34

    Core Word Guide: "In and Out". 36

    Core Word Guide: "Is" 38

    Core Word Guide: "It" 40

    Core Word Guide: "Like". 42

Core Word Guide: "Mine" 44

Core Word Guide: "More" 46

Core Word Guide: "Need" 48

Core Word Guide: "Not" or "Don't" 50

Core Word Guide: "Put" 52

Core Word Guide: "See" 54

Core Word Guide: "Stop" 56

Core Word Guide: "That" 58

Core Word Guide: "Want" 60

Core Word Guide: "What" 62

Core Word Guide: "Where" 64

Core Word Guide: "You" 66

Index 69

Appendix 1 71

Appendix 2 73

Acknowledgments 77

References 81

About the Author 82

Preface

Several years ago, a classroom teacher and I were approached by a parent who asked us if we could attend a particular conference about core words. After the conference, we would then follow this program when working with her son and his AAC system at school. Soon after, both the teacher and I attended this conference and quickly realized that there had been a significant amount of research that had accumulated relating to the relevancy of core words and the impact that they have on both communication and literacy. Just as it does with all children, both literacy and communication go hand-in-hand.

In another classroom, I had a student who had been using a typical communication program for years, but there had not been a specific emphasis with core words. Her literacy skills were not strong, therefore her ability to create sentences on her own, that were not pre-programmed, was difficult. We (this other classroom teacher and I) started emphasizing core words immediately and within weeks "Katie" was starting to form her own phrases with the words that we had introduced so far. Both of these classrooms had children who used AAC systems but who were very different from each other in terms of diagnosis. One classroom had children who had been diagnosed with Autism and the other had children who had a variety of motor and communicative deficits resulting in multiple disabilities. In both of the classrooms, with the children who were targeted, changes with literacy and communication started to occur at a pace faster than I had experienced previously with children who did not have an emphasis with core words.

I did a little research to find the top schools in Michigan that use core words with AAC systems as a program. Two were recommended and one happened to be close to Grand Haven. I contacted the program and they eagerly invited me to come and observe their school. They had been using core words for two years and were seeing great results with both communication and literacy. They then invited me to attend a closed conference where they were having the head of ASHA's (American Speech Language and Hearing Association) Special Interest Group for AAC, Gail Van Tatenhove. Her conference included current research, as well as examples of how to incorporate core words into a daily classroom curriculum both for literacy development and for communication. The ideas for teachers, families and speech-language pathologists were relevant and practical. It didn't necessarily matter what AAC software program was used, just that core words were included and targeted.

That following fall, I returned to my "mentor" school. They gave me permission to take examples of how their teachers worked with core words in the classroom setting. I showed these examples to the teachers, and over the next year, I watched as both teachers used core words daily within their classroom curriculum with their students. Regardless of the communication system that was being used by the child (PECS: Picture Exchange System, eye-gaze systems, basic communication software, strictly core word programs, sign language, etc.), progress with the core words relating to communication and literacy was consistent. Additionally, I worked with parents during the school year on home programs specifically with core word communication. Their interests for the home setting, as well as their feedback, helped me to design additional relevant activities and ideas as the year progressed.

Ultimately, I decided that I needed a program for all of us to work together. However, I could not find any that were appropriate for a variety of ages, that included the use of different types of communication systems, and that provided parent and teacher guides for developing communication. I wanted something that I could give to parents and teachers that would allow them to either use independently or coordinate working together with communication and literacy. I also wanted something that would be helpful for parents and educators who didn't have a great amount of training, if any, in speech and language development and/or the use of AAC systems. I realized that if I wanted a program with all of this, I would need to create one. This is how *Core Words for Classroom and Home* began.

My hope is that this program will be useful for parents, teachers, and speech-language pathologists to help our children communicate at their true level of ability.

A Note to Families, Educators, and Speech-Language Pathologists

This is a Teacher, Parent, and Therapist program for "us," the adults, to help our students and children learn to communicate to their true potential.

The intent of this program is to create a coordinated and meaningful guide, for both at school and at home, so that the adults in both settings can work together, with our children, on *core word* activities that will promote optimal communication. This program ideally is written for both the school and home settings to work together simultaneously. However, if implementation of this program in both settings is not possible, it can easily be practiced in either setting independently.

Over the past several years, with the use of the iPad and touch screens, software programs for communication, as well as the continual advances with technology, we have been able to tap into potential and develop communication skills as never before. For AAC users (Augmentative and Alternative Communication), the research in this area, as well as the experience of therapists, educators, and parents, has allowed us to integrate technology with greater accessibility and more meaning. Still, this is a "young" time in our field. As caregivers, *you* as parents and teachers are the most influential adults, or "therapists," in the lives of your children. You interact with them daily and regularly. Your influence is tremendous, and your potential to help children communicate is often not realized.

The design of this program provides a pathway to practice core words with activities that are predictable, routine and educationally functional (and fun!). With structure, adults can become proficient with strategies that help our children to communicate more effectively. Once these strategies are understood, they can be generalized. Ultimately, as generalization occurs, communication becomes more relevant and powerful, and enables our children to become more connected to their world.

Most important, with all of the activities and emphasis on core words, we must remember that communication and basic social interaction are motivated by true enjoyment. These are not "lessons" to be learned, but opportunities that we the adults are providing, to engage our children with different reasons to communicate with greater intention. Our interactions with our children need to be meaningful and fun, both for them and for us, as "fun" experiences truly engage the mind. An interested mind improves attention, which leads to learning and practice. With shared enjoyment, we create emotional connections that are powerful and motivate our children to take risks to follow our lead.

This program is for the many students and children who need "our" help to learn to communicate so that they may begin to realize their true communicative potential.

Core Words

What Are Core Words?

Core words are the most frequently used words to communicate (Cross, Baker, Klotz, and Badman, 2006). When we study the words that are most common in our daily speech, we find that approximately 80% are "core" words. For example, words such as "it," "that," "want," "more," "do," and "have" are typical core words. The remaining 20% are considered "fringe" words, which are pretty specific (Baker & Hill, 2000). These are words for names of people and places, adjectives (colors, shapes, sizes, etc.) and words that refer to a particular thing (dog, apple, block, school, etc.). There are many more "fringe" words than "core" words within our vocabulary, but our use of words is primarily "core" when we speak and often when we write (Stubbs, 1986).

Traditionally, most of our PECS (Picture Exchange Communication System) and communication software programs have primarily used "fringe," but not necessarily "core" words. This is understandable, as it is difficult to show a picture of "it." However, we use this word quite often. Fortunately, we don't need to reject or change a system, we can just incorporate "core" into what our children are already using, regardless of the system.

The following is an outline that will help us to incorporate both "core" and "fringe" words into our daily communication with our children who are using AAC, learning to use AAC, or maybe are speaking less intelligibly and need assistance with AAC to communicate more effectively.

The Program Outline

The goal of this program is to focus on a particular core word in a structured way that emphasizes different ways to communicate with this word. Every two weeks a new core word will be chosen, ideally to emphasize both at school and at home, that can be practiced within a variety of activities.

This booklet includes an outline of a daily program to use, activities that include the core word, and ways to incorporate that core word both with speaking and AAC. Within this program, there is a *"Core Word Weekly Outline"* that describes how to use the core word each day. Coordinated with this is a *"Core Word Guide"* that describes activities that can be used to help prompt the word at different language levels and within many different formats. Activities include: books (library and online), writing, art, cooking and games.

Before we get started, there are some terms and "teaching practices" to keep in mind that are defined in the pages that follow. It is important to understand the terms that we use in the same way, as well as understand strategies and practices similarly, so that there can be some consistency when working with our children to help them learn to communicate optimally.

AAC—Augmentative and Alternative Communication

Augmentative and alternative communication (AAC)—includes all forms of communication (other than oral speech) that are used to express thoughts, needs, wants and ideas. (ASHA.org).

Augmentative—to help with speaking. With the use of oral speech, we can use AAC to improve speech clarity, or, to help create sentences that may be hard to say. Some of our children "augment" their speech by using a device to say longer sentences, to help create a sentence, or to help make what they say more clear to others.

Alternative—instead of speaking. For many different reasons, some of us cannot speak. We need an "alternative" way to communicate. This can occur in more than one form, as often we combine different AAC systems to become more holistic with communicating efficiently.

Different types of AAC systems can include: sign language, pictures, gestures, facial expression, writing/typing, and the use of a computer device that speaks or has voice output capabilities (i.e., Proloquo2Go, Words for Life, Snap + Core First, etc.). All of these can be used and/or coordinated for optimum communication.

Reasons to Use AAC

There are different reasons to use AAC. A common misunderstanding is that using AAC will "prevent" speech from occurring. Use of AAC often helps people to communicate more effectively if their speech is not sufficient or ideal for their needs. The following are examples of different reasons why AAC may be used.

Not speaking clearly—some children can speak but cannot necessarily be understood. Often, they may use the same words and phrases over and over to respond to questions or just to communicate. Reasons can include: saying words that people understand versus risking not being understood, not knowing how to say something new or more clearly, and eventually maybe just because of habit. AAC can help "push" language so that it is practiced with a visual and auditory cue, which helps with the imitation of words and phrases. Eventually, AAC may not be used or needed at all, as the child has learned how to speak with greater clarity and sentence structure.

Not knowing how to put thoughts into words—some children have a thought, but it doesn't automatically create a sentence in their minds. So, they have to try and think of how to say something. This can be very difficult when it is not automatic. Their words and sentences can be clearly spoken, they just don't know how to create words and/or form sentences. AAC can help to organize simple phrases, practice them, and give a visual cue in addition to hearing a sentence spoken. Some children learn language better with pictures or visual cues. Repetition where they can see, hear and practice something over and over helps with communication.

Not being able to talk—some children are born with a different oral/facial structure or have injuries where the body changes. There may be muscle tone changes, different shapes and sizes of the mouth/face, or nerves that just don't work normally to move the muscles as they should. Some words may be understood, where most are not, or, speaking cannot occur at all. Sometimes the body (arms, legs, body in general) is also affected. AAC can help, as it is used to access the cognitive and communicative potential of the child, regardless of how the body moves or accesses a system to communicate.

Use of Routines to Communicate

One of the best ways to start communicating with AAC and practicing effectively is to use routines. Daily routines help both the student and the parent/teacher practice something new or less familiar. The routine creates predictability—a structured way to practice and build upon for both the child and the adult. Eventually, within the routine activity, communicating becomes more automatic. Once it is automatic, we add another routine. After you have two or three routine activities, spontaneous communication can occur more naturally.

The following are examples of routine activities where we can practice communication daily and with predictability. Initially, it will take more time during these routines to communicate with your child before, during, or after the activity. However, remember that with time it will become automatic and will more easily transfer to other situations for spontaneous communication.

The Home Setting

Common routine activities within the home setting may include: getting dressed, bathing and washing hands, brushing teeth, eating meals and snacks, setting or clearing items from the table, doing household chores, picking up toys or personal items, getting ready for bed, and saying goodnight.

The School Setting

For Younger Children: Common routine activities may include: greeting, circle time (stating name, choosing a song, responding to a routine question, etc.), art activities, sensory play, snack time, reading time, recess or gross motor play, and getting ready for home.

For Older Children: Common routine activities may include: arriving and greeting the class/teacher, requesting help with locker/backpack, preparing and/or requests for snacks and meals, daily interactions or specific activities that occur with each different teacher or subject, regular requests for help or for needed items, preparing for home, and basic expectations for social exchanges with teachers and peers.

Routines offer many possibilities for daily social and communicative exchanges. As communication skills develop, the expectations for phrase length, use of vocabulary, choice of verb tense, and reasons to communicate can be adapted and embedded into the same routine activities.

Things to Keep in Mind*

My first day of graduate school started with a speech. The topic was about children who have severe communication deficits and the importance of the "other half" within the communication exchange. This typically includes the parent and classroom teacher, who spend many hours with the child on a daily basis. Because communication includes two or more people, the effect of the adult's actions and words within that exchange is significant.

When your child learns to speak, you as a parent are there to model the sounds and words to say. As he/she develops language, you change what you model to include more complex words and sentences. You *"match"*—move with the level of your child's abilities. You *"take turns"*—say something and give your child a chance to imitate or respond. We must do the same when communicating with AAC. It is a back and forth communication system where the parent/teacher models what the student needs to do to communicate, then gives him/her an opportunity to respond or imitate. We cannot give someone an AAC system and expect them to communicate effectively without our guidance. As we are models with words and sentences verbally, we need to be with our children's AAC systems. We need to use these systems regularly as we interact with our child or student.

Remember that keeping things fun and interesting for both you and the child truly matters. Following are some helpful strategies to keep in mind when interacting with your child or student.

Match. Doing something or saying something at the same level as your child's skill level, or one "step" above. Match not only their abilities but also their interests.

Turntaking. The back and forth nature of an interaction where each person takes a turn either when speaking and/or in action. This allows modeling of how to communicate or "act" by the adult and then opportunities to imitate and practice by the child. Turntaking is the foundation for basic conversational exchanges that we have with others.

Balance. Doing about the same as each other on each of your turns. Make sure your turns are equal, or "balanced." Allow each other to do about the same amount of speaking and/or action on each of your turns. Remember to wait quietly and "with expectation" for your child or student to respond. Waiting quietly for 5, 10 or even 20 seconds may seem "long", but it may be what the student needs to make his/her response to take their turn.

---

*Referenced from *The Eco Model,* by James D. MacDonald, PhD.

Sensitive Responsiveness. Watching and listening closely for those little changes in attention, interest and ability, etc. Knowing when to prompt your child, when to wait more, when to move ahead and/or when to give a break. Watch closely how the child looks at things, prepares his/her body to respond, and processes (thinks about) what is said or modeled by the adult.

Emotional Attachment. This is the bond that motivates us. The emotional attachment that develops between the adult and the child can be tremendously motivating and powerful. It is important to engage in activities that encourage positive communicative exchanges. Often, we become so focused on specific outcomes and goals that we neglect to think about the real emotional exchange that occurs within each adult-child interaction. The type of emotional attachment the student has with the adult can have a great impact on the child's decision to take risks and to keep trying when something is difficult.

Use of a Prompt Hierarchy

A prompt hierarchy is used to gradually decrease the amount of "help" that the adult gives the child to communicate, either verbally and/or with an AAC system. The hierarchy is a system to help fade the prompts in a gradual and predictable way so that speaking and/or use of AAC becomes more spontaneous. Cued-dependency (waiting to act or communicate until someone prompts in a certain way) can be a very difficult system to "un-do." Often, students learn how to use a communication system with the adult setting up all of the activities and then cuing the child for when and how to communicate. For some students, these cues and the set-up of communication exchanges becomes expected as part of the process to communicate in general. The prompt hierarchy decreases how much help we as adults give our children, in a gradual way, so that they will continue to have success when communicating. Use of a prompt hierarchy system can be key to helping a child to become a competent communicator. As adults, we need to think about how much we are "helping" or "prompting" and determine when and how to reduce our cues. The following is an example of a hierarchy system that can be used (*adapted from PRC's AAC Language Lab*).

Most Direct to Least Direct

Level 5: *Direct Model*—The adult/communication partner says and/or demonstrates (on the device or with a sign) how to say the word or phrase and waits expectantly for the child to imitate. Help is given as needed.

Level 4: *Partial Verbal Prompt or Gesture*—The adult partially models how to create a phrase or use a word. The adult/communication partner says part of the phrase or beginning of the word, then waits for the child to finish or imitate. For AAC, point to the core word or symbol on the AAC system that is being used.

Level 3: *Written Prompt*—The adult/communication partner writes down (i.e. dry erase marker on a white board) the word or phrase to be spoken with an expectation for the child to repeat. Practice two or three times; then take away the written cue and have the child try to do and/or say it again.

Level 2: *Request a Response or ask an Open Question*—The adult/communication partner may say "Tell me what you want" or asks a question "What do you want?" and waits for the student to respond.

Level 1: *Environmental Cue*—The desired item/activity is available to be seen or understood in some obvious way but the adult waits before responding so that a communicative interaction occurs (i.e., snack is left on the table) so that the child/student must make a request.

The Core Word Program

How Do We Do This?

On the following pages is the Core Word Program. It includes the *Core Word Weekly Outline*—which is a daily schedule for both school and home, 2 weeks in length, which gives an outline of what to do each day regarding how to prompt and use the targeted core word. Following the Core Word Weekly Outline are the *Core Word Guides*—these are the individual core words, each with a "guide," which gives specific suggestions to show how to use that particular core word within phrases and activities. The guides are made for a variety of different ages, interests, and language abilities. Use the *Core Word Guide* for the entire two-week session, and follow the *Core Word Weekly Outline* that shows what to do each day for those two weeks.

On the second page of each guide is a picture of the core word in two AAC software programs that have been commonly used over the past several years and in sign language. These include Prentke Romich Company's Words For Life, Proloquo2Go (AssistiveWare's Crescendo Core 7x11) and commonly used signs from ASL (American Sign Language*). Of note, these are just examples and not meant to be exclusive of any other program or company.

Included at the end of this booklet are 1) *Reasons to Communicate*—a list of different reasons we communicate to help promote more functional communication and 2) *Core Word Phrases*—a list of approximately 80 core words with phrases that can be used to communicate with each word.

The Program's Core Words (listed alphabetically):

Do	In/Out	Put
Finished/All Done	Is	See
Get	It	Stop
Go	Like	That
Have	Mine	Want
He/She	More	What
Help	Need	Where
I	Not/Don't	You

*Referenced from ASL by LifePrint

Core Word Weekly Outline

Note: Present the core word 3 consecutive times, at school and/or at home, when saying, signing and finding/typing the core word. The adult says it, signs it, and locates it on the AAC system with the child imitating each step. If a student does not use AAC, he/she can type it. Then after this has been done 3 times, go around the classroom/family and give each child or family member a chance to say, sign, and locate the core word on the AAC system. For non-AAC users, write or type the word on a laptop, paper or computer system.

WEEK 1

Monday: The new core word is presented to the class/child: *Say* the core word, then *Sign* the core word, then *Find* the core word (on AAC program). Have the class or your child imitate this back to you each of the three times. Even if there is no AAC program, you can write or type the core word. Make sure you model the word (say it clearly and show where to find it, sign it, and/or write it), and give your child/students a chance to imitate. Practice by taking turns around the classroom or at home saying, signing, and locating/typing the core word. Then, write one or two short phrases with the core word: "I _____ _____" (i.e., I like it, I want it, I do it...). Again, practice by taking turns around the room or at home saying the phrase (verbally and/or with AAC).

Tuesday: With the targeted core word—Say it, Sign it, Find it, and Write it/Type it again as on Monday three times. Have the class or your child repeat after you each of the three times. Create short phrases (use the '*Phrases*' from your "*Core Word Guide*"). Practice making phrases and saying them together and/or individually around the classroom or with the family.

Wednesday: With the targeted core word—Say it, Sign it, Find it, and Write it/Type It, again three times. Read a book (online or from the library/etc.) from the "*Core Word Guide*" suggestions. Have the class read the book with you (overhead with the class, or one-on-one at home). On each page that has the core word, practice saying and finding the word on the AAC device. At home, read the story and find the core word, taking turns locating it on your child's device. Try to say or create some of the phrases from the book, with the core word, by modeling for the child with an opportunity for him or her to imitate.

Thursday: With the targeted core word—Say it, Sign it, Find it, Write it/Type it, again three times. Repeat Wednesday's plan. Practice the book again and expand with questions if the class/child can find and/or say the words easily. Create phrases and questions about the book using the core word.

Friday: With the targeted core word—Say it, Sign it, Find it, Write it/Type it, again three times. Do an activity with the class or at home. Choose a game, an art, or a cooking activity that emphasizes the core word from the "*Core Word Guide*." Use the core word in many different types of phrases during the activity. Have your child/student create phrases to ask questions and to respond using the core word (with family at home or with class peers). Help by modeling how to say and/or use AAC to create a word or phrase, at their level of ability or one step above. *Remember to have fun throughout the activity; try not to lose focus that the actual outcome is not as important as your interactions together. Model language and offer opportunities to imitate.*

> **Note:** *During week 2—start to really use the core word in phrases with your classroom and/or with your child and family at home. Try to make comments, ask questions, respond to questions and emphasize the core word regularly so that the child can listen to lots of different ways to communicate with that one word. Offer opportunities to have your child imitate as able.*

WEEK 2

Monday: With the targeted core word from the previous week, Say it, Sign it, Find it, Write it/Type it again three times as in the previous week. Both you and your student(s)/child should be finding it and/or saying it more easily now. Repeat Tuesday from Week 1 practicing phrases from the "*Core Word Guide.*" Pair up with a partner and practice asking and responding to questions with the phrases. You are "refreshing" your memory from the prior week.

Tuesday: With the targeted core word—Say it, Sign it, Find it, Write it/Type it again three times. Read the book from week 1 (or choose another book) and create phrases (questions, comments, rejection) to expand on different reasons to communicate. Look at the "*Reasons to Communicate*" section at the end of this book for additional ideas to communicate. Or, try a *Writing* activity that can be practiced again on Wednesday (see writing activity below on 'Wednesday').

Wednesday: With the targeted core word—Say it, Sign it, Find it, Write it/Type it again three times. Practice a written activity from the "*Writing*" section on the "*Core Word Guide.*" Help the class/your child come up with ideas to fill in the responses to the writing activities. You may need to write down ideas that your child can then choose from to help respond to the writing activity questions/ideas.

Thursday: With the targeted core word—Say it, Sign it, Find it, Write it/Type it, again three times. Play a game or do another activity in the "*Ideas*" section of the "*Core Word Guide.*" Or, read another story or create a classroom/family story with the Tar Heel Reader. Have your child choose an activity from several that you have pre-selected (book, game, online activity, writing something together…). When playing a game, try to incorporate different phrases with the core word as much as possible. Remember to wait for your child or student to imitate; allow time for processing and for trying to communicate.

Friday: With the targeted core word—Say it, Sign it, Find it, Write it/Type it, again three times. Do an activity with the entire class or in small groups, or, at home. Use a game, a cooking, or an art activity from the "*Core Word Guide.*" Help your child by breaking down the cooking or art activity into small steps. Think in terms of opportunities to ask questions, make requests, and make comments using the targeted core word. Most of all . . . have fun!!

Core Word Guides

On the following pages, 24 core words are presented alphabetically, each with its own Core Word Guide. Each of these Guides includes a variety of activities that target that particular core word. Included within each activity are examples of phrases that can be used to promote communication verbally and/or with AAC programs.

Each guide includes a list of Phrases for that core word, Literacy materials (print books and online books), Writing activities, Games and Ideas, Art activities and Cooking activities. Following the cooking activities are screenshots of two common core word software programs. Each screenshot provides a short description of where to locate that particular core word on the software screenshot.* Finally, the targeted core word is presented at the bottom of the page in sign language following an American Sign Language (ASL) format. All of these activities and descriptions of where to find a core word on a device and how to sign it are so that the adult can prompt the student in a variety of ways to further develop their understanding and use of each core word.

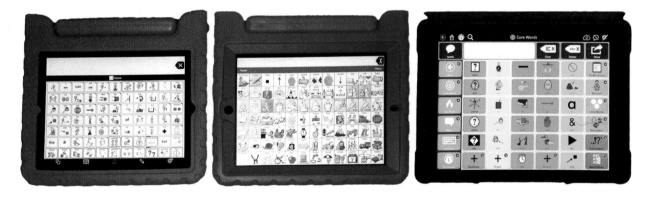

Shown above are three current software programs that are used to target core words. These include (from left) AssistiveWare's Crescendo 7x11 home in Proloquo2Go, Prentke Romich's Words for Life One Hit 84, and Tobii Dynavox's Snap+ Core First.

---

*Please note: The examples of the software screenshots shown on the Core Words pages are not meant to promote a particular company's program, or exclude another company's materials. Of note, there are many different software programs that can include core words, and changes in software and design happen quickly and continuously.

Core Word Guide: "Do"

Phrases: I do it, You do it, Do you want it?, Do you want more?, Do you have _____?, Don't do that/it, Do you like it?, Can I do it?

Books/Literacy: The following books have repeated lines with the word "do":

• *What Do People Do All Day*, by Richard Scarry

• *I Can Do It*, by Little Golden Books

• *Brown Bear, What Do You See?*, by Bill Martin, Jr.

• *What Do You Say?*, by Mandy Stanley

• *Mr. Brown Can Moo, Can You?*, by Dr. Seuss

Online: Try these Tar Heel Readers:

https://tarheelreader.org/2018/07/30/do-it/

https://tarheelreader.org/2018/03/30/what-do-you/6/

https://tarheelreader.org/2018/01/21/what-do-you-see-10/6/

Writing: Write a list of things you like to do—"I like to do _____," Write to a class-mate—"What do you like to do?" and take turns asking and responding in writing.

Games/Ideas: Many games can include the word "do": Go Fish—"Do you have?, I do have a _____, I do not have a _____," Memory—"I do/do not have a match." Many activities that we do throughout the day use the word "do." Look for opportunities during the day to model "do." Here are some examples: Cooking, e.g. "Do that, I can do it," Packing up, e.g., "You do it," Hygiene, e.g., "I can help you do it, Do it now," etc.

Art: Make *Molding Clay!* Create a batch of plain clay and separate it into different containers to make different colors (add food coloring and mix/knead). Store in containers that are airtight or use Ziploc bags. Recipe for "uncooked" dough: 2 cups self-rising flour, 2 Tbs alum (grocery store spices section), 2 Tbs salt, 2 Tbs cooking oil, 1¼ cups boiling water. Mix together and wait to set. Ideas: Make pancakes with different toppings, little animals, faces with different emotions, etc. Prompt: "I do like that, I do not like this, Do you want more _____?, What do you like?, Do you have _____?" etc.

Cooking: *Make Pancakes!* Make a batch by following a recipe on a box or from scratch (I cup flour, I cup milk, 1 tsp baking soda, ½ tsp baking powder, 2 Tbsp sugar, 1 egg, ¼ cup melted butter or oil). Take turns asking about toppings or ingredients to add in the pancakes: blueberries, chocolate chips, cinnamon, strawberries, syrup, whipped cream, jam… (*Gluten, egg and dairy-free*: www.floandgrace.com/2010325saturday-pancakes-gfcf-and-egg-free-html/) Prompt: "Do you want _____?, Do you like _____?, I do/do not like _____, Do you have more _____?" etc.

LAMP WFL: Do—Finger with string—
Fifth row, 7th button

Proloquo2Go (Crescendo Core) 77:
Do—First row, 5th button

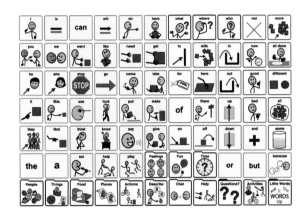

Sign: Do—Make a side-to-side motion from left to right with both hands slightly cupped.

Core Word Guide: "Finished, All Done"

Phrases: It is all done/finished, I am finished/all done, Are you finished/all done?, When are we all done/finished?, She/he is finished/all done, We are all done/finished!

Books/Literacy: The following resource has repeated lines with the words "all done/finished":

Online: Try this Tar Heel Reader: it emphasizes the word "finished/all done"

https://tarheelreader.org/2018/07/04/finished-all-done/

Writing: Write a list at the end of the class session or school day, or, at home after school or in the evening after completing some errands, tasks, games, etc. with each other. Make a list with "finished" or "all done": "I finished _____" (art work, a story, an athletic activity, something at lunch, math class, etc.), "I am all done with _____."

Games/Ideas: Games: With any game, whoever finishes first, has an opportunity to exclaim "I am done!" There are many opportunities during the day when "all done or finished" can be used. Prompt: "I am done/finished, We are done/finished" when completing school assignments, either individually or as a group, when finished eating/drinking, when finished with a small break, when finished doing a task at home (folding something, making a bed, handing dishes to someone or cleaning up, etc.). As adults, model "I am done/finished" as we complete things. Ask "Are you done?" and wait for the child to respond.

Art: *Salty Ceramics!* Mix 1 cup salt, ½ cup cornstarch, ¾ cup of water then place over heat or in a microwave on medium-low. Stir constantly on the stove and take quick breaks to stir if in the microwave. Mixture is done when it thickens into a white blob the size of an orange. Remove from heat and place on foil, knead until soft. Sculpt any object and add feathers, pebbles, beads, shells, toothpicks, etc. while still soft. Once dry, coat with glaze or a fingernail polish! Prompt: "I am done/finished, Are you finished/all done?"—while touching or pointing to something," I am all done/finished with (name sculpted object or art item being used to sculpt), When will you be done with this?" etc.

Cooking: *Make 'Paradise Punch'!* Mix the following ingredients: One 6 ounce package cherry Kool-Aid (unsweetened), 1½ cups sugar, 2 quarts of water, 6 ounces frozen orange juice (prepared according to directions), 64 ounces 7-Up, Sprite or Squirt. Place in a large bowl and serve with a scoop of vanilla ice cream in your cup! Prompt: "Are you finished/all done?, It is all done/finished, I finished it, Did you finish?, Is it all done?" etc.

LAMP WFL: Finished—Boy with book—
First row, 1st button

Proloquo2Go (Crescendo Core) 77:
All Done—Second row, 11th button

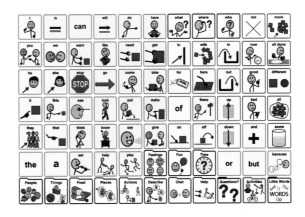

Sign: Finished/All done—Place both of your open hands in front of you, palms facing you, with fingers facing upward. Then, twist both hands quickly a couple times (or once) ending with the palms pointing away from you or forward.

Core Word Guide: "Get"

Phrases: Get that, Get it, Go get it, What did you get?, Get it now, Get it later, Get more, I got it

Books/Literacy: The following books have repeated lines with the word "get":

• *Dear Zoo,* by Rod Campbell

• *Shoes from Grandpa,* by Mem Fox

Online: Try this Tar Heel reader: it emphasizes the word "got"

https://tarheelreader.org/2018/07/29/what-do-you-get-2/

https://tarheelreader.org/2015/05/22/we-went-to-the-grocery-store-2/15/

Writing: "I got _____," "I get _____," "She gets _____," "We will get _____." Write a list of things you need to get, e.g. to make something, or to go somewhere.

Games/Ideas: Talk about things you need to "get" to go somewhere, e.g. going outside? "Get" your coat; going shopping? "Get" your money; playing soccer? "Get" your ball. During active play, give directions, such as: "Get in, Get out, Get up, Get down, Get off, Get on," etc.

Art: *Make Pasta Pictures, Models, or Jewelry!* Make pictures using dried (uncooked) pasta. Use different shapes and sizes. Draw a circle on a paper and fill in with pasta eyes, hair, ears, etc. Glue pasta pieces together to make people, animals, or monuments, etc. String penne, rigatoni, macaroni, agnelli, tortellini, or tie farfalle with little knots and let dangle. You can paint the pasta first, then arrange how you would like. Prompt: "Get more _____, I get the _____, Did you get the _____?, What did you get?, Let's get more," etc.

Cooking: *Make Pasta!* Place cooked plain pasta in different bowls to try different flavors: Choose a pasta (*Gluten-free—rice, bean, or corn pasta*). Use ramen noodles in the microwave (follow the steps in the recipe) or make your own on the stove! Help to remove the pasta with a slotted spoon or tongs if pouring water out of the pot seems too difficult. Try different flavors in each bowl; olive oil with salt, add fresh or dried basil, try another with sage, add tomato sauce in another, add a meatball with sauce in another, try a cream sauce in another… Talk about the different tastes, shapes and/or ingredients. Prompt: "Get the _____, (salt, oil, sauce…), I got it, I got the _____, Let's get more _____, What did you get?" etc.

LAMP WFL: Get—Sunshine with mountain—Fifth row, 9th button

Proloquo2Go (Crescendo Core) 77: Get—Second row, 6th button

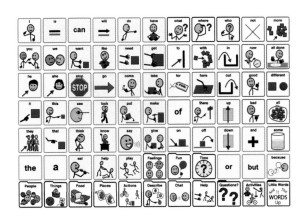

Sign: Get—Start with your hands slightly open claw shapes and held away from the body, then pull your hands back towards your body as they close. They become "S" hands in ASL.

Core Word Guide: "Go"

Phrases: Go, I go, You go, Don't go, I want to go, Go now, I go now, You go now, Do you want to go?, Where are we going?, Let's go

Books/Literacy: The following books have repeated lines with the word "go":

• *Go, Dog. Go!*, by PD Eastman

• *Go Away Big Green Monster*, by Edward R. Embeley

• *Will You Please Go Now*, by Dr. Seuss

Online: Try these Tar Heel Readers:

https://tarheelreader.org/2018/07/30/go-stop/

https://tarheelreader.org/2018/03/17/where-do-you-go/

https://tarheelreader.org/2015/03/31/go-not-go/

https://tarheelreader.org/2014/06/03/some-dogs-go/

https://tarheelreader.org/2016/06/28/go-5/

Writing: I go to _____," "I went to _____," "I want to go to _____," "I go in a _____."

Games/Ideas: Card games/ board games—say "go," or "I go," "you go" to request or take a turn during the game During cooking lessons, use "go," as you turn on blenders, start stirring, turn on the microwave, set the timer for the oven and more. Racing/running/walking/riding/pushing—Use and model "go" during these activities.

Art: *Paint with Marbles or Straws!* Place three marbles in a foil pie plate or cookie sheet with sides, tape or glue white paper to the bottom of the tray. Place three colors of tempera paint (primary colors) on the paper in different parts of the tray. On the word "Go" place the marbles in the pan and roll them around, making different colors with the streaks. Or, with older children, use straws and on the word "Go" blow the paint through the straw to see how it moves on the paper. Thin the paint with water if needed. Talk about the changes with the colors, new colors formed. Prompt: "Go, You go, I go, I go now, He goes, She goes, Who goes?, Go more?, Look at it go," etc.

Cooking: *Make Cookies!* Follow a recipe on a box (can be gluten-free) or make some from scratch. Here's a basic recipe where frosting and sprinkles/decorations can also be added: 1 cup sugar,

1 cup butter, 1 egg, 1 tsp vanilla, ½ tsp salt, 1 tsp baking soda, ½ tsp baking powder, 2 cups flour (or more if needed). Mix the sugar and butter together (blend with a mixer or stir by hand), add the egg and stir, add the dry ingredients and stir. Bake at 375 degrees for 10–12 minutes, then decorate with icing and sprinkles once cooled. Prompt: "Go!" To turn on the mixer or to stir, to add the next item (pour, crack egg, mix). " I go, You go, Go now, Go more, Can I go?, Do you want to go?" etc.

Lamp WFL: Go—Frog jumping—Fifth row, 8th button

Proloquo2Go (Crescendo Core) 77: Go—Green arrow—Third Row, 4th button

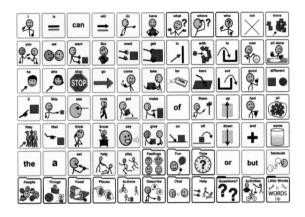

Sign: Go—Point your index fingers up in both hands and quickly move them forward together until pointing away from yourself. The motion is in the wrists.

Core Word Guide: "Have"

Phrases: I have it, Do you have a __?, What do you have?, We have a _____, I have to _____, I have to go

Books/Literacy: The following books have repeated lines with the word "have":

• *The Lunch Box Surprise*, by Grace Maccarone

• *Have You Seen My Cat?*, by Eric Carle

Online: Try these Tar Heel Readers:

https://tarheelreader.org/2018/07/29/in-the-morning-i-have-to/

https://tarheelreader.org/2018/07/29/i-have-8/

https://tarheelreader.org/2017/08/17/have-2/

Writing: Write a list of things you have in your lunch bag, in your bedroom/classroom, in your backpack. Past tense: "If I had a _____, I would _____ it." (e.g., "If I had a cookie, I would eat it," "If I had a cat, I would pet it"...)

Games/Ideas: *Go Fish*: "Do you have _____, No, I don't have _____, Yes I do have _____." *Memory:* "I have a match, I don't have a match, I have the same cards, I have different cards, What do you have?", *Hi Ho Cheery O:* "What do you have?"

There are apps where you can make silly photos: Use photos of students/people and add extra features, or do their hair. Model "I have _____," e.g. "I have green hair," "I have glasses," etc.—Toca Hair Salon Me: itunes.apple.com/au/app/toca-hair-salon-me/id730873197?mt=8—Party face: itunes.apple.com/au/app/party-face!/id593062627?mt=8

Art: *Make Sculpture Dough Animals!* Use pre-made arts and crafts dough with different colors, or follow this cooked clay/dough recipe: I cup flour, I/2 cup salt, 1 cup water, 1 Tbsp cooking oil, 2 tsp cream of tartar. Mix and add food coloring if you would like. Heat in a pan or electric skillet until the ingredients form a ball. Allow to cool. Before mixing together, separate the ingredients and name what each of you have: "I have oil, I have flour," etc. You can make different animals. After making and requesting, describe your animal. Prompt: "I have a _____ (name the animal), What do you have?" "I have two _____ (legs, eyes, ears, label body parts)," "Does it have a _____ (tail, legs, ears)?" etc.

Cooking: *Make Animal Biscuits!* Use pre-made biscuit dough from the refrigerator section in the grocery store. Take two to three biscuits and make the body and then face of the animal (dog, cat, bear, bird, fish..). Take another biscuit and separate it into different body parts—roll out tails, legs, whiskers, eyes, ears, etc. Bake the biscuits then coat with a mixture of brushed on melted butter, cinnamon sugar and honey. Talk about what you "have" on your biscuit. Prompt: "What do you have?, Can I have more?, I have two _____ (ears, eyes, wings...), I have to make a _____," etc.

LAMP WFL: Have—Money—Fourth row, 7th button

Proloquo2Go (Crescendo Core) 77: Have—First row, 6th button

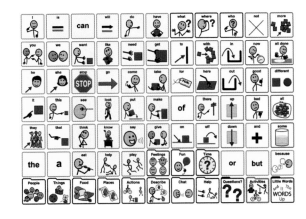

Sign: Have—Hold "bent" hand-shapes a few inches out from your upper chest then move your hands back and touch your chest.

Core Word Guide: "He & She"

Phrases: He/she is _____, He/she likes it, He/she likes _____, He/she wants it, He/she wants _____, He/she feels _____, Where is he/she?, She/he goes now.

Books/Literacy: The following books have repeated lines with the words "he & she":

• *He Bear & She Bear*, by Jan and Stan Berenstain

• *Oh Dear*, by Rod Campbell

• *There Was an Old Lady Who Swallowed a Fly*,

• *Matilda's Cat*, by Emily Gravett

• Fancy Nancy books, by Jane O'Connor

• Charlie & Lola books, by Lauren Child

• Spot Books by Eric Hill

Online: Try these Tar Heel Readers:

https://tarheelreader.org/2018/04/14/he-is-she-is/

https://tarheelreader.org/2018/04/14/who-is-it-he-or-she/

https://tarheelreader.org/2016/12/09/we-sit/

https://tarheelreader.org/2017/01/02/we-feel-3/

https://tarheelreader.org/2016/06/20/what-we-like-3/

Writing: Write phrases using photos of people, pets, book characters, etc.: "He is _____," "She can _____." Write a list of things friends and family can do, "He can _____, She has _____, He likes _____, She likes _____, etc.."

Games/Ideas: Model "he" and "she" during any activity to describe what students can do, e.g., He can sing, She can jump, He can draw, She can laugh, etc. He/she can + any verb. Model he and she during any activity to describe things about students, e.g., He is funny, She is silly, He is tall, She is pretty. Take turns describing what you see in photos e.g., He is running, She is swinging, He is eating, etc.

Art: *Draw an Outline of a Boy or Girl on Colored or White Paper!* Label it as a boy or girl, so that during the activity you can talk about "he" or "she," ("She has _____, or, He has _____"). Color in eyes, hair, clothing, etc. with colored pencils, paints and or markers/crayons. If you want, take turns drawing the picture together. One person does the eyes, another the hair, the arms, the legs, etc. Taking turns drawing one picture together helps with sustained attention. Talk about your pictures using 'he' and 'she' throughout the activity. Prompt: "She has _____ (brown, green) eyes, He has a _____ (striped shirt), She has _____ (red hair, blue teeth), Is he _____ (happy, sad), Is she done?" etc.

Cooking: *Decorate Sugar Cookies with Icing of Different Colors and/or Sprinkles!* Make boy and girl faces while labeling what feature each has: "She has blue eyes, he has brown hair, she is silly, he is happy… Make sure you label the cookie as a boy cookie face or a girl cookie face so that the "he and she" make sense. Prompt: "She has _____ (brown hair, big teeth, long hair), He is _____ (silly, surprised), He has _____ (freckles, spiked hair), Is he finished?, Is she done?" etc.

LAMP WFL: He/She—Faces of boy and girl, He—Fifth row 2nd button, She—Sixth row, 1st button

Proloquo2Go (Crescendo Core) 77: He/she—Third row, 1st and 2nd buttons

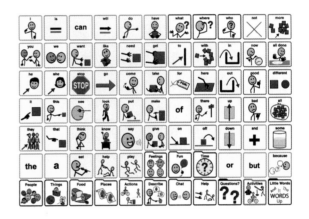

Sign: He/She—In ASL to indicate He, She, or It you just point at the person or thing to which you are referring.

Core Word Guide: "Help"

Phrases: Help, Help me, I want help, I need help, Do you want help?, Please help me, Help me _____, Don't help me, I don't want help, Can you help me?

Books/Literacy: The following books have repeated lines with the word "help":

• Henry Helps books, by Beth Bracken

• *Cook It*; *Fix It*; *Grow It* books in the Helping Hands series, by George Birkett

• *Help! I Really Mean It*, by Lauren Child

• There are many titles around occupations, e.g. People Who Help Us

Online: Try these Tar Heel Readers:

https://tarheelreader.org/2018/07/30/help-me-2/

https://tarheelreader.org/2016/07/27/police-are-here-to-help/

Writing: Write sentences such as: "I help to _____," "_____ helps me when I'm _____," "She helps to _____," etc.

Games/Ideas: The concept of "help" is important when teaching self-advocacy. Model "help" regularly whenever you see a student/child struggling with a task. Give the student/child a chance to ask for help, by presenting opportunities to them when they need help. For example, give them unopened yogurt, screw a lid on too tight, place a ball out of reach, etc.

Art: *Carve a Pumpkin*! Gather a child-friendly knife for pumpkin carving (grocery store), a marker and a pumpkin. Draw a face together on the pumpkin (take turns with the eyes, nose, teeth, top near the stem..). Carefully use the knife and carve out a face. Prompt: "Help, help me draw, help me do the ____ (eyes, teeth, top…), Do you want help?, Can you help?, I don't need help," etc.

Cooking: Bake *Pumpkin Seeds!* Take your pumpkin seeds and rinse them through a strainer to get the gooey pumpkin slime off of them. Place the seeds in a bowl and drizzle oil or melted butter on them, stir to coat. Place the seeds on a cookie sheet and salt lightly. Bake at 300 degrees for 45 minutes or until golden brown. Prompt: "I need help, Can I help?, Do you want help?, Can you help me?, Help me _____ (open, turn, get it…)," etc.

LAMP WFL: Help—Bathtub picture—
Fifth row, 12th button

Proloquo2Go (Crescendo Core) 77:
Help—Sixth row, 4th button

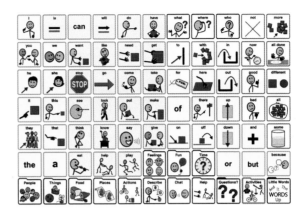

Sign: Help—Make a fist with your right hand placing the thumb to the side of the fist vs. in front of the fingers (make an "A" in sign). Place the outstretched palm of your left hand under the right hand and raise both hands. You may also reverse your hands so that the left makes an "A" sign and the right hand is under the left.

Core Word Guide: "I"

Phrases: I, I do, I do it, I want _____, I want it, I like it, I don't like it, I go, Can I _____?, I am _____ (adjective, feeling), I see a _____, I see it

Books/Literacy: There are many books with repeated lines that begin with "I" or some other form of first person singular, including:

• *I Went Walking*, by Sue Williams

• *Come Out and Play*, Little Mouse, by Robert Kraus ("I can't play today")

• *Here Are My Hands*, by Bill Martin Jr. and John Archambault

• *Green Eggs and Ham*, by Dr. Seuss ("Sam I Am")

• *Are You My Mother*, by P.D. Eastman

• *Dear Zoo*, by Rod Campbell

• *Brown Bear, Brown Bear*, by Eric Carle

• *What Do You Like?*, by Michael Grejniec

Online: Try these Tar Heel Readers:

https://tarheelreader.org/2018/02/12/what-do-you-like-8/7/

https://tarheelreader.org/2018/02/02/i-want-fruit/6/

https://tarheelreader.org/2018/01/21/what-do-you-see-10/9/

Writing: Write sentences such as: "I like _____," "I go _____," "I see _____," "I play _____," "I have _____," and many more.

Games/Ideas: *Spot It*: "I see a _____," *I Spy*: "I spy something _____." Explore what students like. Model "I like _____" during class/home discussions for things you like and then give students a turn to finish the sentence. Take photos of things you like or places you go and create a class/family book: "What I like, Where I go." Talk about places you go. Model "I go _____" during conversations about places you go and then give the student/child a turn to finish the sentence or imitate on his/her turn.

Art: *Make Lake Michigan Waves!* Make a wave bottle with an empty water or pop bottle. Using a funnel, fill the bottle 1/3 with water and add a preferred food coloring (blue is common, but any will be fun). Then add oil (canola, mineral, vegetable) almost to the top. If you leave a little room, you can also add glitter and then top off the rest of the bottle with more oil. Seal the lid by adding glue around the top edge or around the inside of the cap. Place it on the bottle and close tightly. Now you have a wave bottle! Have your child make requests by giving him/her choices. Prompt: "I want _____ (color, art item like glue, glitter, water, oil, bottle…), I see _____, I like the _____, I need more _____," etc.

Cooking: *Make a Banana Shake!* Use bananas (1 to 2), 1 cup ice, ½ cup milk, 2½ tsp sugar or honey, 1 scoop vanilla ice cream, 1½ tsp vanilla extract (optional) and if you want, add some chocolate syrup to make it a banana chocolate shake! Place all ingredients in a blender. *Casein-free*—substitute orange juice for milk, omit the ice cream and yogurt and add berries instead! Prompt: "I do it, I want a turn, I would like _____ (banana, chocolate…), I want _____ (ingredient…), I like it, I don't like it, I want more," etc.

LAMP WFL: I—Girl, Third row, 1st button

Proloquo2Go (Crescendo Core) 77: I—First row, 1st button

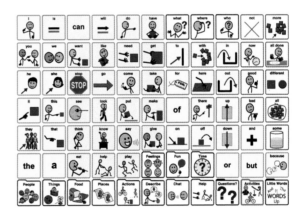

Sign: I—Touch your chest with your index finger.

Core Word Guide: "In and Out"

Phrases: Go in, Go out, Put it in/out, Want in/out, I want it in/out, In here, In there, Go in/out, Come in/out, That is in/out, It is in/out, Not in here, Is it in?, Is it out?

Books/Literacy: The following books have repeated lines with the word "in or out":

• *Who Sank the Boat?*, by Pamela Allen

• *Dog In, Cat Out*, by Gillian Rubinstein

Online: Try these Tar Heel Readers:

https://tarheelreader.org/2018/07/29/in-and-out-single-words/

https://tarheelreader.org/2018/07/29/in-and-out-4/

https://tarheelreader.org/2012/03/07/in-my-pocket/

Writing: Use sentences with in and out, e.g. "He went in/out _____, It was in _____, I put in the _____, I took out the _____." Have a grab bag, pull something "out," and write what you took out: "I took out a _____."

Games/Ideas: There are many activities/games where objects are put in and taken out of things. Look for opportunities to model "in" and "out" with games, e.g. Connect 4, basketball, Singing the "Hokey Pokey" song. During many activities we do throughout the day, we can model "in" and "out," look for opportunities throughout your day to use them. Here are some examples: Cooking? "put in bowl, take out of the oven"; Lunchtime? "take out yogurt, put in the bag"; Backpacks? "put that in, take it out"; Shopping? "put in cart, take out, put in bag, take out of bag," etc.

Art: *Sort Items!* Grab 3 to 5 bowls and place them on a table. Find items that have different attributes that can be sorted by color, function, or some similarity that is obvious. Gummy bears can be sorted by color, blocks can be sorted by color or shape, pictures can be sorted by animals, toys, people, or a particular concept. Foods can be sorted by fruits, vegetables, dairy, sweets, etc. Move from simple to more complex over time. Place an item in a bowl to show what should be matched. After you are done, take the items "out" of the bowls and put them away. Prompt: "Put it in, Take it out, This goes in, _____ goes in, They are out, Does it go in?, Does it go out?" etc.

Cooking: *Make Lemonade!* Follow directions on a packet, or, use real lemons, sugar and water! Wash 2 to 3 lemons, roll them on a counter pushing down with your palm until slightly soft (makes the juice come out better). Help cut the lemons in half, use a lemon reamer (handheld juicer for oranges, lemons, etc.) to remove the juice from the lemon halves. Add 4 to 8 cups water to a pitcher, ½ cup sugar (more to taste) and stir until the sugar is dissolved. Pour over ice cubes in a cup and add a lemon wedge for fun! Prompt: "Put it in, put _____ (lemons, juice, ice, water…) in, Put more in, Pour it out, Pour juice out, Pour more out, Do you want more in?" etc.

LAMP WFL: In—Bridge—Second row, 8th button; Out—Can with blocks—First row, 10th button

Proloquo2Go (Crescendo Core) 77: In—Second row, 9th button; Out—Third row, 9th button

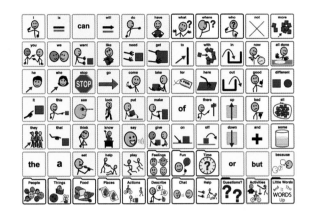

Sign: In—Right hand goes into cupped left hand.

Sign: Out—Right hand comes out of cupped left hand.

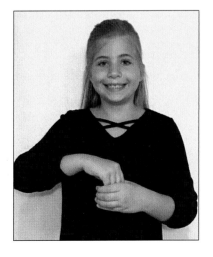

Core Word Guide: "Is"

Phrases: It is mine, It is yours, Is it good?, It is _____ (adjective such as color, temperature, size), It is a _____ (name of something—a picture, something on the table at the meal, label something you see…) What time is it?, What is it?

Books/Literacy: The following book has repeated lines with the word "is":

• *Today Is Monday*, by Eric Carle

Online: Try these Tar Heel Readers:

https://tarheelreader.org/2018/07/30/what-is-it-14/5/

https://tarheelreader.org/2018/07/30/what-is-it-14/7/

https://tarheelreader.org/2015/04/04/eating-5/

Writing: Use sentences to describe a picture such as: It is a _____, She is _____, He is__, Is he/she __ (sad, running…), Is it a____? Look on a Calendar—"Today is _____ (Monday, Tuesday…), The month is _____, Tomorrow is _____," etc.

Games/Ideas: *I Spy:* "Is it a _____?, It is a _____," *Memory:* "It is a _____," *Zingo:* "This/that/it is a _____." Talk about the day and month using a calendar: "Today is Monday, It is February…" Emphasize "is" when speaking the day and month. Practice taking turns with questions such as: "What is your favorite color?" where students in the classroom or family at home ask each other questions.

Art: *Make Gak!* This is a "dry-like" slime that you can make into any color. Get a bowl and mix the following: 4 oz. white glue, ½ cup *warm* water, food coloring (any color several drops), and 1 teaspoon borax (you find this in the grocery store with the powdered laundry detergents). Mix all together and you will soon see it form into a semi-solid slime that can be rolled, pushed, pulled and formed into a ball. Take turns mixing the ingredients and talking about the gak. Prompt: "It is _____ warm, gooey, blue, soft…, Is it my turn?, Is it your turn?, It is your turn…, It is gross/yucky, it is nice," etc.

Cooking: *Make Pizza!* Use refrigerator biscuit dough (or gluten-free) and create a pizza together. Make a 'healthy' one (olive oil, spinach, Parmesan cheese), traditional (tomato sauce, mozzarella cheese, pepperoni), or a fun one (bbq sauce, chicken, onion and cheese optional). Take turns adding items, tasting, and describing the pizza ingredients. Prompt: "It is _____ (sweet, round, cheese, big, hot, finished…"), Is it done?, What is that?, My pizza is _____ (good, funny, hot, done)," etc.

LAMP WFL: Is-Bucket—Third row, 4th button

Proloquo2Go (Crescendo Core) 77: Is—First row, 2nd button

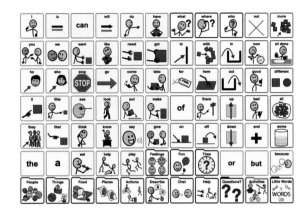

Sign: Is—Place the edge of the right hand crooked index finger on chest, move forward a couple of inches. Of note, there is no sign in ASL for "is." This is the sign used in *Signing Exact English,* another sign language program.

Core Word Guide: "It"

Phrases: It is mine, It is yours, I want it, Do you want it?, It is good/bad, Do you have it? I have it, I like it, I see it, Is it mine?

Books/Literacy: The following books have repeated lines with the word "it":

• *Dear Zoo*, by Rod Campbell

• *It Looked Like Spilt Milk*, by Charles G. Shaw

• *David Gets in Trouble*, by David Shannon

Online: Try these Tar Heel Readers:

https://tarheelreader.org/2018/01/20/zoo-what-is-it/6/

https://tarheelreader.org/2018/02/12/do-you-like-it/5/

https://tarheelreader.org/2012/03/01/party-food/10/

Writing: "It is _____," "It was _____," "I like it because _____." Write a sentence at the end of a lesson, school or home activity or the end of the day. A simple sentence such as "It was a _____ day (good, bad, sad, fun…)." At home, take turns so that each of you can express an idea in a sentence.

Games/Ideas: Bingo/Zingo, Memory: "It is the same, It is different, I have it, Did you get it?"…, Spot It—"I see it!" Use "it" with many different games and activities. Going shopping? "Put it in" (the cart); Need help? "Get it" to reach something too high; Need more to drink? "Pour it in"; Do you like it? "I like it/I don't like it." When getting dressed, making something to eat, putting something down or on a shelf, use "it" in phrases to model the many ways "it" is used.

Art: *Make Homemade Paint!* Mix 2 Tbsp of sugar with ½ cup cornstarch. Slowly add 2 cups of cold water and cook over low heat, stirring constantly until mixed well. Pour into separate cups/bowls and add food coloring to make different colored paints. Paint on waxed paper or plain white paper. Prompt: "It is _____ (color, cold, warm,), It needs more _____, I like it, I don't like it, Do you like it, What do you like?" etc.

Cooking: *Make a Caramel Fondue with Apples!* Cut apples into slices. Combine a 5 ounce can of evaporated milk, 1 cup brown sugar, 2 Tbsp butter, and bring to a boil in an electric skillet or pan on the stove. Turn off the heat and mix for one minute. Pour the fondue into separate bowls for dipping apple slices and enjoy! *Casein-free*—substitute caramel with honey and cinnamon, mix together and drizzle on the apple slices! Prompt: "It is sticky, It is sweet, It is good/bad, It is mine/ yours, Is it done?, It looks _____ (add an adjective), Do you like it?, What do you like?" etc.

LAMP WFL: It—Sheep—Fifth row, 1st button

Proloquo2Go (Crescendo Core) 77: It—Fourth row, 1st button

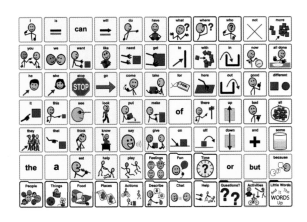

Sign: It—In ASL to indicate He, She, or It, you just point at the person or thing to which you are referring

Core Word Guide: "Like"

Phrases: I like _____, I like it, You like it?, Do you like it? I don't like it, I would like more _____, I would like to _____.

Books/Literacy: The following books have repeated lines with the word "like":

• *Green Eggs and Ham*, by Dr. Seuss

• *What Do You Like?*, by Michael Grejniec

• *I Really Like Slop*, by Mo Willems

• *Maisy Likes Driving*, by Lucy Cousins

• *I Like Books*, by Anthony Browne

• *Run Like a Rabbit*, by Alison Lester

• *Things I Like*, by Anthony Browne

• *You Choose*, by Pippa Goodhart & Nick Sharatt

Online: Try these Tar Heel Readers:

https://tarheelreader.org/2018/02/12/what-do-you-like-8/

https://tarheelreader.org/2015/12/05/spot-the-dog/

https://tarheelreader.org/2018/02/12/like-4/5/

https://tarheelreader.org/2011/11/07/chocolate-11/

Writing: Use sentences such as: "I like _," "I don't like _____," "She likes _____," "He doesn't like," etc. Make a list of groceries, art supplies, birthday items you would "like," "I like to have _____," I like _____." Make a list of foods that you do not like—"I don't like _____."

Games/Ideas: After reading a book, discuss what part of the story you "like." Discuss what character you "like" and why. Discuss what character you did "not like" and why. With picture books, talk about the pictures (what is happening, what you see). Talk about things you would "like" to get for a birthday or an important event or activity.

Art: *Make Fruit Murals!* Cut fruits in half, stick toothpicks or forks in the "non-flat" end and use tempera paint or water colors to paint on white paper, construction paper, etc. Use apples, pears, grapes, berries, kiwis, oranges, etc. Dip the fruit in the paint tray so that the flat side is dipped into the paint, then place on the paper to make a fruit print. Talk about colors and shapes with like and don't like. Prompt: "I like _____ (fruit name, I like it, I like _____ (blue, red, green... then name the fruit), Do you like it?" etc.

Cooking: *Make Fruit Salad!* Make a salad with fruits you "like"—apples, grapes, oranges, pears, strawberries, blueberries, kiwi, etc. Talk about the flavors of different fruits and take turns talking about what you "like" or "don't like." For added flavor, combine plain yogurt with some brown sugar and vanilla. Mix into the fruit to add sweetness. Prompt: "I like the _____ (name fruit), I like _____ (sweet, tart, juicy, mushy...), What do you like?, Do you like _____ (name a fruit)," etc.

LAMP WFL: Like—Sunshine—4th row, 5th button

Proloquo2Go (Crescendo Core) 77: Like—Second row, 4th button

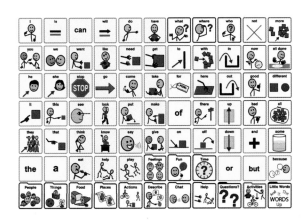

Sign: Like—Move the hand forward while bringing the index and thumb together.

Core Word Guide: "Mine"

Phrases: It is mine, Is it mine?, That is mine, Yours or mine?, Can I have mine?, Where is mine?, Do you have mine?, Mine is here/there

Books/Literacy: The following book has repeated lines with the word "mine":

• *Mine!,* by Shutta Crum

Online: Try this Tar Heel Reader:

https://tarheelreader.org/2018/07/30/it-is-mine/

Writing: Have the students/your child make a list of things that he/she owns: "Things that are mine: _____." Make a list of items that can include books/videos/movies, school supplies, clothing items, games/toys/sports equipment, etc. Pair up with a student or at home and make a list to share with each other.

Games/Ideas: Many activities during the day can use the word "mine." At school there are pens, pencils, computers/chromebooks, water bottles, etc. where there may be multiples within the room. Create opportunities to emphasize times during the day where the question is asked "Whose is this?" when pointing to or holding something, so that a response such as "That/it is mine" can be practiced. At home, during meals, in shared spaces where there are similar items (toothbrushes, drinking cups, clothing items, etc.) questions can be used to prompt responses with "Mine." "Whose milk is this?, Whose shoes are these?, Whose book is this?," etc.

Art: *Salad Spinner Art!* Gather paper, tempera paint and a plastic salad spinner. Place paper at the bottom of the spinner (cut to size of the spinner bottom). Drizzle some tempera paint onto the paper with a spoon, use more than one color if desired. Place the basket into the spinner, snap the lid on and spin! Watch as the paint splatters within. Thin the paint with water if needed. Open and place the paper on a surface to dry. Prompt: "Mine is next, Is it mine?, Where is mine?, Do you have mine?, When do I do mine?" etc.

Cooking: *Make Cheese Quesadillas!* Get some corn and/or wheat tortillas, either small/or large in size. Sprinkle cheese of your choice on top of the tortilla—Colby, American, Mexican blend, cheddar, or a mix of several! Warm the tortilla in either a microwave or skillet on the stove. Place on a plate and eat as is with the melted cheese, or add extra ingredients such as black beans, tomatoes, cilantro, sour cream/plain Greek yogurt, some salsa, etc. Prompt: "Whose is this?—while pointing or holding something to elicit "It is mine!," ask "Is this mine?" when holding yours or another's item, grab the wrong item so that the student/your child can say "That is mine," etc.

LAMP WFL: Mine—Envelope with pencil—
First row, 2nd button

Proloquo2Go (Crescendo Core) 77:
Mine—Proloquo2Go does not have "mine" programmed into Crescendo Core 77.
It needs to be added by the user.

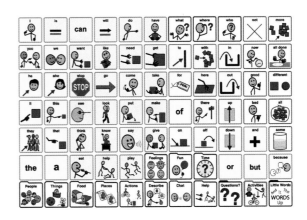

Sign: Mine—Place your flat hand on your chest and tap your chest twice.

Core Word Guide: "More"

Phrases: More, I want more, No more, I don't want more, Do you want more?, Does he want more?, One more, One more time

Books/Literacy: The following books have repeated lines with the word "more":

• *More Spaghetti, I Say*, by Rita Golden Gelman

• *More Pants*, by Giles Andreae

• *Guess How Much I Love You*, by Sam McBratney

• *Ten Apples Up on Top*, by Dr Seuss

• *More Bears*, by Kenn Nesbitt

• *Just One More*, by Jennifer Hansen Rolli

Online: Try these Tar Heel readers:

https://tarheelreader.org/2018/02/25/more-12/

https://tarheelreader.org/2018/03/04/more-that/

https://tarheelreader.org/2018/02/25/do-you-want-more-breakfast/

https://tarheelreader.org/2018/02/25/do-you-want-more/

Writing: Use sentences such as: "I like more _____," "She wants more _____," "There are more _____." Write a list of what you need "more" of in the classroom—food, materials, pens, paper, art supplies, etc.

Games/Ideas: Create opportunities to model "more" by only giving a small amount of something (an item or an action) to a student, then wait to see if he/she wants more. Some simple ideas include: Pouring juice into a cup, Swinging with one or two pushes (then stop), Blowing bubbles/balloons—blow a little then stop, Music—play a little then stop, Drawing—give one color versus the whole box. Wait. Then prompt a phrase with "more" if needed.

Academically, you can work on the concept of "more" during class/home activities. Model "more" as you put together groups of objects or when counting. Compare groups of items and discuss which one has "more"; during a snack or meal, which plate, bowl or cup has "more," etc.

Art: *Make Bird Treats*! Take a slice of bread and cut out a shape with a cookie cutter (optional). Make a hole in the top and tie with a string so you can hang the treat later. Or, find a pine cone and tie a string from the top. Brush the bread/pine cone with the egg white or peanut butter, sprinkle on birdseed and then allow to dry a few minutes. Walk outside and find a tree from which to hang the bird treat so that you can see it from a window! Prompt: "'More birdseed, I need/want more _____ (bread, pine cones, peanut butter, birdseed), I need more _____ (shapes to use), Do you want more?" etc.

Cooking: *Make Popcorn Balls or Sweetened Popcorn*! Make microwave, air pop or stove top popcorn. Mix together: ¼ cup melted butter, ½ cup brown sugar, ½ cup Karo syrup and salt to taste. Drizzle over the popcorn and eat, or make popcorn balls once the syrup mixture is cooled enough to handle safely. Yum! Prompt: "I want/need more _____ (popcorn, syrup, sugar), I want to eat more, more popcorn?, do you want more?" etc.

LAMP WFL: More—Hands with musical notes—Fourth row, 10th button

Proloquo2Go (Crescendo Core) 77: More— First row, 11th button

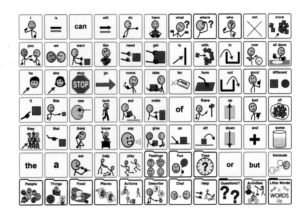

Sign: More—Use flattened "O" hands and bring both hands together.

Core Word Guide: "Need"

Phrases: I need help, What do you need?, I need a _____, I need more, I need more _____, Do you need more?, They need a _____, He/she needs a _____.

Books/Literacy: The following books have repeated lines with the word "need":

• *The Pigeon Needs a Bath,* by Mo Willems

• *Monster Needs a Party,* and other Monster books, by Paul Czajak

• *Wombat Stew,* by Marcia K. Vaughan

• *Have You Seen My Potty?,* by Mij Kelly and Mary McQuillan

Online: Try these Tar Heel Readers:

https://tarheelreader.org/2018/07/30/need-2/

https://tarheelreader.org/2016/05/01/looking-after-dogs/

https://tarheelreader.org/2016/04/21/wants-and-needs-9/

https://tarheelreader.org/2016/03/21/needs-or-wants/

Writing: Create sentences such as: "I need a _____," "I need to _____," "He/She needs to _____." Help your child or the class come up with topic ideas to write about. For example, for birthdays and holidays: Make a list of things you "need" to get: "For my birthday, I need _____"; "We need to get _____," "For Thanksgiving, we need _____," etc.

Games/Ideas: Plan an event or activity where a list of things you "need" is made: Going shopping? "I/we need _____; Making arts and crafts? "I need _____ (paper, markers, paint...); Cooking? ""I/we need _____ (eggs, sugar...), etc. Prompt: "I need _____, We need _____, What do you need?, I need more _____, Do you need more?

Art: *Make Cinnamon Ornaments!* 1 cup cinnamon, $2/3$ cup applesauce, 1 Tbsp white glue. Mix the ingredients together in a bowl until a stiff dough forms. If it is too thin, add cinnamon. If too dry, add applesauce. Using a rolling pin, roll the dough out to about ¼ inch on a floured surface. Cut out shapes with cookie cutters and place on a cookie sheet. Make a hole in the top (with a pen/pencil) for the string. Allow to dry for 24 to 48 hours, or, bake at 250 degrees until they are hard (around 25 minutes). Decorate when cool with fabric paints in squeeze bottles. Prompt: "I need _____ (cinnamon, spoon, more, name a cookie cutter shape...), Do you need more?" etc.

Cooking: *Make Butter Cookies!* 2 cups flour, ½ tsp salt, ¼ tsp baking powder, 1 cup butter (2 sticks), 1 cup sugar, 1 egg, 1 tsp vanilla. Beat the sugar and butter, add the egg and mix together. Add the vanilla and mix, then add the dry ingredients and mix with a spoon. Either drop a spoonful onto a greased cookie sheet, or, form 2 logs rolled in waxed paper and chill. Cut the rolls in ½ inch sections and place on a greased cookie sheet. Bake at 375 degrees for 10–12 minutes. Prompt: "I need _____ (sugar, butter, more, the mixer…), I need that, Do you need that?, Do you need more?" etc.

LAMP WFL: Need—Umbrella—Seventh row, 8th button

Proloquo2Go (Crescendo Core) 77: Need—Second row, 5th button

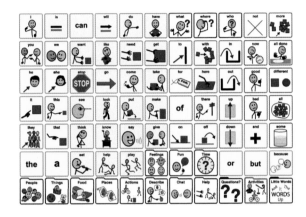

Sign: Need—The movement is downward. Starts and ends in an "X" handshape (index and middle finger crossed). Movement is mainly in the wrist and not the arm.

Core Word Guide: "Not" or "Don't"

Phrases: I do not like, I don't like, I do not/don't want _____, Not here/there, Don't go, Don't stop, Now now

Books/Literacy: The following books have repeated lines with the word "not":

• *Go, Dog, Go!*, by P.D. Eastman ("Do you like my hat? I do not.")

• *Ten Apples Up On Top!*, by Theo. LeSieg

• *Green Eggs and Ham*, by Dr. Seuss

• *That's Not My …* books, by Fiona Watt

• *Waiting Is NOT Easy*, by Mo Willems

• *But Not the Hippopotamus*, by Sandra Boynton

• *I Will Never Not Ever Eat a Tomato*, by Lauren Child

Online: Try these Tar Heel Readers:

https://tarheelreader.org/2018/07/29/dont-do-that-2/6/

https://tarheelreader.org/2018/02/12/do-you-like-3/4/

https://tarheelreader.org/2018/02/12/do-you-like-it/9/

https://tarheelreader.org/2015/03/31/you-can-open-or-not/

https://tarheelreader.org/2015/03/31/go-not-go/ /

Writing: Use "not" in lots of different sentences to describe preferences about an activity or book in class or home. "I do not like _____," "She did not want/like _____," "It is not _____," etc.

Games/Ideas: *Go Fish game*—"I do not have…," *Memory*—"I do not/don't have it." The concept of "not" can be difficult to understand. Model "not" when your child/student is upset, protesting, or refusing something. The child does not need to repeat you during these moments. "You do not like that, you are not happy, you do not want to go." Prompt "not" by giving the wrong item—for example, give the wrong type of juice, give a spoon instead of a fork, give the wrong book or item to a class activity. Use things that are obvious to the student so that they clearly know it is "not" right.

Art: *Make Clear Spheres!* Mix 3 cups of water (distilled is better than tap, but tap works), 1 cup of dish soap (Dawn or Joy are good—try not to use an "Ultra" dish soap), and 1 tsp of glycerin (local pharmacy). Use a straw or wand and dip it into the solution, then make a "sphere" by blowing slowly. Store in a container with a lid overnight and it will be even better! Blow slowly to make large spheres, fast to make lots of small ones. Take turns back and forth. Prompt: Don't stop, Do not blow fast/slow, That is not big/small, You don't blow—I blow, I don't go,—you go, Don't you want more?" etc.

Cooking: *Make Dog Bone Cookies (really for dogs)!* 1 egg, 1 cup water, 2 Tbsp honey, 1 cup peanut butter (natural best)—mix these together. Then add: 1 tsp baking powder and 2½ cups flour. Mix the dry ingredients with the wet. You can drop and flatten a cookie on the sheet, or, roll them out and use different shaped cookie cutters. Bake at 350 degrees for 20 minutes until golden. Use lots of core words with this activity, but focus on "not" and "don't." During the activity, prompt: "Don't you want more?, I don't want to eat that!, I don't want more, I don't like that," etc.

LAMP WFL: Not—Rope with Knot—Seventh row, 2nd button

Proloquo2Go (Crescendo Core) 77: Not—First row, 10th button

Sign: Not—Place the thumb under your chin and move hand forward a few inches.

Don't—Move hands from center (crossed) to sides.

Core Word Guide: "Put"

Phrases: Put it down, Put it there, Put it in, Put it here, Where did you put it?, Where do I put it?

Books/Literacy: The following books have repeated lines with the word "put":

• *Wombat Stew*, by Marcia K Vaughan

• *Ten Apples Up on Top*, by Dr. Seuss

• *Put Me in the Zoo*, by Robert Lopshire

• *Don't Put Your Finger in the Jelly*, By Nick Sharatt

Online: Try these Tar Heel Readers:

https://tarheelreader.org/2018/07/30/put-3/

https://tarheelreader.org/2014/09/28/fruit-22/

https://tarheelreader.org/2015/02/26/salad-2/

Writing: Write phrases such as "He put on _____," "She put it in _____," "I put _____ in my bag." Write lists of things to "put" in your backpack, or things to "put" in your lunch bag: "Put in a banana, put in cookies, put in a sandwich…, things to "put" on your pizza or salad, etc.

Games/Ideas: Mr. Potato Head—Put the _____ in (ear, arm, eyes), Puzzles, Play-Doh. Arts and crafts? "Put it on/in…"; Cleaning up? "Put that away, Put that in"; Dressing? "Put shoes/shirt on"; Daily activity "Put toothpaste on."

Art: *Plant Flowers or Veggies!* Get a plastic cup and make holes in the bottom for water to drain (2 to 3 will do). Place potting mix in the cup ¾ full, add a flower/veggie or a seed of a flower/veggie and place about ½ inch into the dirt. Carefully water the plant. If it is a seed, keep a sheet of plastic wrap over the top of the cup and keep the dirt moist. Wait 2 to 3 weeks for it to germinate. This is a great opportunity to offer choices to your child, either with actual plants (during the spring is good) or with seed packets. They can make more than one cup and then plant the flower/veggie outside if frost is not a concern. Prompt: "Put in some _____ (dirt, water, name of plant), Put more in, What will you put in?, I am putting in _____," Where do I put it?" etc.

Cooking: *Make Brownies (from a box or from scratch)*! Decorate the brownies with frosting and add sprinkles. Prompt: "Put in the _____ (egg, flour, mix, chocolate, butter, oil…). Put on more _____ (frosting, sprinkles, other decorations), Where do I put it/that?" etc.

LAMP WFL: Treasure chest—Put—Sixth row; 12th button

Proloquo2Go (Crescendo Core) 77: Put—Fourth row; 5th button

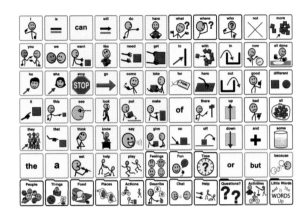

Sign: Put—The pad of your thumb is pressed up against the underside of the fingers as if you were holding onto a piece of cardboard and "putting" it somewhere. A flattened "A" or "O" hands in sign.

Core Word Guide: "See"

Phrases: I see it, I see a _____, I see _____, What do you see?, I don't see it, Do you see it?, See you later, I want to see it

Books/Literacy: The following books have repeated lines with the word "see":

• *I Spy* books by Edward Gibbs

• *Can You See What I See?* books by Walter Wick

• *Brown Bear, Brown Bear, What Do You See?,* by Bill Martin Jr/Eric Carle

• *Walking Through the Jungle*, by Debbie Harter

• *Peepo*, by Janet Ahlberg

Online: Try these Tar Heel Readers:

https://tarheelreader.org/2017/12/06/i-see-33/

https://tarheelreader.org/2018/01/21/what-do-you-see-10/

https://tarheelreader.org/2018/01/20/i-see-a-colors/

https://tarheelreader.org/2018/01/20/on-the-farm-i-see/

https://tarheelreader.org/2017/12/06/i-see-33/

https://tarheelreader.org/2018/01/20/in-my-classroom-i-see/

Writing: Write the phrase "I see (a) _____"when looking around the room. You can write the specific thing you see ("I see a _____"), or, describe it i.e., "I see (something) red," or "I see (something) big and blue…" Or, choose from several pictures or objects and write what you see.

Games/Ideas: Play "I Spy," model "see" as you find things "I see something _____," Play "Spot It" using the phrase "I see a _____." When out in the community, model "see" as you notice things while riding in the car, when taking a walk, going to the zoo, or on a field trip. Prompt: "What do you see? I see a _____." Take turns so that you can model to the child different ways to respond.

Art: *Glue Art!* Lay out waxed paper. Using white glue, make shapes that are thick in form (stars, circles, animals, people…). You can use cookie cutters if you would like! Wait for the glue to dry, then color the forms with markers. Or, color your glue ahead of time by mixing it with tempera paints. Use separate containers for each color. Once dry, peel the glue forms off of the waxed paper and lace with thread, ribbon, string or yarn. Hang wherever you like! Prompt: "See it?, What do you see?, I see a _____, I see the color _____," etc.

Cooking: *Make Sugar Cookies*! Before baking, separate and place the dough into different bowls. Using food coloring, create different colored cookies as drop cookies or from cookie cutters. Or, make a large rainbow cookie by putting the colors next to each other in an arch. Follow a recipe on a box (good for gluten-free) or make from scratch. Omit the colors if there is sensitivity to food coloring, and talk about what you "see" by the different shapes made by the cutters, or, create your own! Prompt: " I see _____ (name colors, shapes of cookie cutters), Do you see the _____? (Name something you are looking for), I see you made a _____," etc.

LAMP WFL: See/Look (2 hits)—Eye—Sixth row, 2nd button; Sixth row, 9th button

Proloquo2Go (Crescendo Core) 77: See—Fourth row; 3rd button

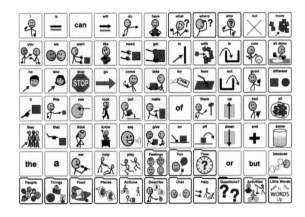

Sign: See—Make a "V" with your fingers with your palm facing in and move forward away from your face.

Core Word Guide: "Stop"

Phrases: Stop it, Stop that, I want to stop, Do you want to stop?, We need to stop, Don't stop

Books/Literacy: The following books have repeated lines with the word "stop":

• *I Can't Stop Hiccuping*, by Lauren Child

• *Stop that Cow*, by Mairi MacKinnon (Usborne First Readers)

• *Red Stop, Green Go*, by PD Eastman

• *Stop Following Me, Moon*, by Darren Farrall

Online: Try these Tar Heel Readers:

https://tarheelreader.org/2018/07/30/go-stop/

http://tarheelreader.org/2016/06/29/the-walking-song/

http://tarheelreader.org/2015/09/20/stop-it/

Writing: Write sentences such as: "I stop and _____," "She stops _____," "They will stop _____."

Games/Ideas: Games: Freeze! (use "stop" instead). There are many activities/games where you can model "stop." Here are some examples: Swinging—stop the swing as you model "stop." Racing, running, walking, riding, pushing—model "stop" at the finish line. Music—model "stop" to stop the music when dancing/moving. During cooking activities, use "stop" as you turn off blenders, when it is time to stop stirring, when the microwave or timer finishes, stop mixing, stop pouring, stop decorating.

Art: *Make Suncatchers!* Get some old (or new) crayons and shave them with a handheld grater (non-electric) or handheld pencil sharpener. Make different colors of crayon shavings and place them between 2 waxed paper sheets cut to the same size and shape. Place some newspaper or a brown paper bag onto a counter, put the waxed paper crayon sheets on top, then place another paper on top of these. Or, use a brown paper grocery bag and place the waxed sheets inside. Flatten and set your iron to "warm" (do not use steam). Press onto the paper with the iron and underneath the crayons will start to melt. Once cool, cut the shapes you would like to make (circles, diamonds, hearts…), punch a hole in the top and hang with a string. You can hang them on a window or from the ceiling. Talk about "more" and "stop" when adding colors. Ask when to "go" or to "stop" throughout the activity when making colored shavings, when pressing the iron, when making different types of shapes. Prompt: "Stop that, Stop it, When do I stop?, Can you stop?" etc.

Cooking: *Make a Shake!* Use ice cream (favorite flavor), milk, and a flavoring such as chocolate, vanilla, strawberry, mint, etc. *Casein-free*—make a fruit smoothie with orange juice, bananas, strawberries and ice! Using a blender, take turns putting in the ingredients and mixing. For older children, work with measurements, and have them say "stop" when 1 cup of juice or milk are poured, or 1 to 2 tsp of flavoring are used, etc.. Prompt: "Stop—no more _____ (orange juice, bananas, berries, ice cream, milk, etc.)" when filling the blender. Say "Stop—my turn, Do I stop?, Can I stop?" etc.

LAMP WFL: Stop—Stop Sign—Fourth row, 12th button

Proloquo2Go (Crescendo Core) 77: Stop—Third row, 3rd button

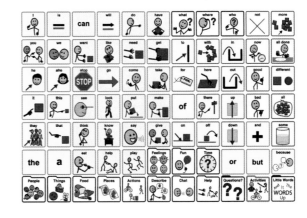

Sign: Stop—Extend your left hand, palm upward then sharply bring your open right hand down to your left palm at a right angle.

Core Word Guide: "That"

Phrases: Get that, That is mine, That is good/bad, I want that, Look at that, Do you want/like that?

Books/Literacy: The following books have repeated lines with the word "that":

• *That's Good, That's Bad*, by Margery Cuyler

• *The Doorbell Rang*, by Pat Hutchens

Online: Try these Tar Heel readers:

https://tarheelreader.org/2018/07/29/that-4/

https://tarheelreader.org/2018/02/03/what-do-you-want-2/6/

https://tarheelreader.org/2018/07/29/dont-do-that-2/

https://tarheelreader.org/2015/11/14/what-if-everyone-did-that/

Writing: Make a list of things that were done throughout the day. Next to each item write a short phrase stating how you felt about the activity—"That was good, That was fun, That was silly, That was bad…" Use photos to describe what you see—"That is _____ (describe the color, size," "That was/is _____" (silly, funny, sad, good—describe the feeling about something just read or seen).

Games/Ideas: Talk about things that you need or would like when out and about—e.g. While taking a walk outside—"I like that," while pointing to a flower. While going shopping—"I want that" while pointing to a food or an item; When choosing a game to play—"(Let's) play that." With board games, point to areas of the board or cards that need to be chosen and model "That is yours, Oh no, you got that?, What did that say?" etc.

Art: *Make Crystal Balls!* Find some Styrofoam balls of different sizes (Meijer's, Hobby Lobby, etc.). Brush them with white glue, sprinkle them with one or more colors of glitter, or roll them in paint, and place them on a tray or foil to dry. Hang them with ribbon or string by tacking the ribbon onto the top of the ball (flat, metal thumbtack). Tape them from a bedroom ceiling, near a window, or in line with a light to see the glitter sparkle. Prompt: "I like that, I want that, That is good, More of that, That is done, Can I have that?" etc.

Cooking: *Make Homemade Granola*! 3 cups oats, 1/2 cup oil (sunflower, canola, etc.), ⅛ cup honey, 1/2 tsp cinnamon, cranberries or raisins, almonds are optional. Over low heat in a sauce pan combine the oil and honey until warm but not simmering. Pour over the oats (and nuts if using) and mix in a bowl. Shake in the cinnamon and mix again until coated. Spread the oats/almonds onto an ungreased cookie sheet and bake for 20 to 30 minutes at 300 degrees or until lightly browned. Stir occasionally while in the oven. Take out of the oven and let cool. Once cool, mix in the cranberries or raisins. Place in an airtight container for two to three weeks. Enjoy with yogurt, as a cereal, mixed with berries, or just as a snack by itself! Prompt: "I like that, What is that?, Do you want that?, That is ____ (sweet, crunchy), That goes in" etc.

LAMP WFL: That—Wizard—Second row, 6th button

Proloquo2Go (Crescendo Core) 77: That—Fifth row, 2nd button

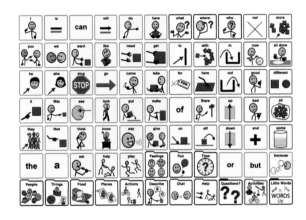

Sign: That—Extend right pinky and thumb straight with the other fingers bent closed. Bring your hand down to the open left hand with the palm facing up.

Core Word Guide: "Want"

Phrases: I want, I don't want, I want it, I want that, I want more, I want help, I want to go, I want to make a _____, I want some _____, I want to play _____, I want to eat/drink _____, Do you want it?, What do you want?

Books/Literacy: The following books have repeated lines with the word "want":

• *The Pigeon Wants a Puppy,* by Mo Willems

• *I Want _____* (Little Princess books), by Tony Ross

• *I Want a Pet,* by Lauren Child

• *Room on the Broom,* by Julia Donaldson

• *I Want to Play Music Too,* by Lauren Child

Online: Try these Tar Heel Readers:

https://tarheelreader.org/2016/09/26/i-want-6/

https://tarheelreader.org/2018/02/02/i-want-fruit/

https://tarheelreader.org/2018/02/02/i-want-16/

https://tarheelreader.org/2018/02/03/what-do-you-want-2/

Writing: Create sentences such as: "I want to _____ (choose an activity), "She wanted a _____ (respond to a question from a book), "I want to be a _____ (add a profession)," "I want a _____ (gift idea, food choice,)" etc.

Games/Ideas: When making choices or requesting things "want" can easily be prompted. Take turns making choices and modeling "I want that!" as you choose an object, food, color, activity, etc. Ask the student/your child to talk about what he/she "wants" during meals, games, books, art and crafts, etc. Allow opportunities to respond to what the child "wants" to do next—"I want _____" (TV show, movie, activity).

Art: *Make Veggie Prints!* Find some cheap wrapping paper and roll it out so that the plain/white side is facing up. Grab some vegetables from your refrigerator and cut them in half (onions, peppers, carrots, `potatoes, corn on the cob, broccoli, celery, etc.). Use tempera paint, pour some colors into individual containers, and place the flat end of the veggie into the paint then press and hold 1 to 2 seconds on the paper. Watch your shapes appear, using different colors. Prompt: "I want

_____ (veggie, color, request for a turn), I want that, I want it, Do you want it?, Do you want more?, Do you want that?" etc.

Cooking: *Veggies and Dip!* Pull some veggies from the fridge, wash them, then cut them up and place them on a plate/tray. Use carrots, cauliflower, celery, snow peas, broccoli, etc. Buy some hummus or make a dip using 1 cup plain Greek yogurt and a tablespoon of dehydrated onion soup mix (from package), or make your own hummus: 1 cup canned chickpeas (drained), ¼ cup tahini, 1 to 2 Tbsp olive oil, garlic to taste (powdered if fresh is too strong), salt and pepper to taste. Mix these and refrigerate, then enjoy your veggie dip! Prompt: "I want _____ (name veggie, ingredient to make or dip), I want more _____-(veggie, flavor in dip), I want to cut, slice, dip, eat.., Do you want it?, Do you want more?" etc.

LAMP WFL: Want—Boy with striped shirt—
Fifth row, 3rd button

Proloquo2Go (Crescendo Core) 77:
Want—Second row, 3rd button

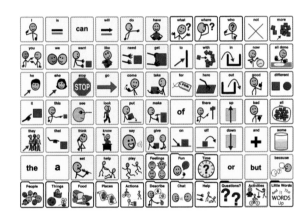

Sign: Want—Palms up and open/flat. Bring the hands back toward you and slightly bend the fingers.

Core Word Guide: "What"

Phrases: What?, What is it?, What do you have?, What do you want?, What is that?, What are you doing?

Books/Literacy: The following books have repeated lines with the word "what":

• *Brown Bear*, Eric Carle

• *Polar Bear*, Eric Carle

Online: Try these Tar Heel Readers:

https://tarheelreader.org/2018/03/30/what-is-it-13/

https://tarheelreader.org/2018/03/30/what-do-you/

https://tarheelreader.org/2018/03/31/what-jokes-to-make-you-laugh/

https://tarheelreader.org/2018/03/31/what-what/

Writing: Write about something you did earlier in the day, and use the following heading: "What I _____ (ate, played, read)." These are examples of topics you can write about. At home, do the same. Take turns writing with your child: "What I _____"(ate at lunch, where you went, what event was fun, what was learned or talked about in school…). Make a list of things you would like or want: "What I like"—then list items on a grocery list, presents for something special (birthday or holiday), something you would like to do (go to the zoo, go bowling, do some coloring).

Games/Ideas: Bingo/Zingo, Memory, Hi Ho Cheery O—Prompt: "What is it?, What do you have?, What number?"

Art: *Create Shiny Paint*! Use liquid tempera paint, corn syrup (drizzle in the paint) and dishwashing liquid (just a few drops). Mix these together and place different colors in separate containers. With a paintbrush make pictures on thick paper (construction, card stock). Dip a string into the paint, fold the paper in half, and move the string out zigzagging slowly to make a design. Paint on white tissue paper to make your own wrapping paper. Prompt: "What is next?, What do you want?, What is it?" etc.

Cooking: *Make Puppy Chow!* Use ½ cup butter, 1 cup creamy peanut butter, 2 cups milk chocolate chips, 1 pkg (17.5 oz.) crispy corn and rice cereal, 1 pound confectioner's sugar. Melt the butter, peanut butter and chocolate together. Pour over the cereal and toss until it is mixed. Place the cereal in a large paper sack, add the confectioner's sugar, fold down the top and shake to coat. Make half the recipe if you'd like. Prompt: "What is next?, What do you have?, What is it?, What do I do?" etc.

LAMP WFL: What—Question mark—
Second row, 9th button

Proloquo2Go (Crescendo Core) 77:
What—First row, 7th button

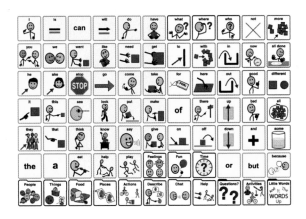

Sign: What (2 versions)—Open hands with "what's up?" expression, or point with your right hand to the left open hand, and starting near the left thumb, drag the tip of your right index finger downward, across the left palm.

Core Word Guide: "Where"

Phrases: Where?, Where is it?, Where do I/we go?, Where did it go?, Where are we/they?, Where do you want to go?, Where is he/she?

Books/Literacy: The following books have repeated lines with the word "where":

• *Where's Spot?* by Eric Hill

• *Where the Wild Things Are*, by Maurice Sendak

• *Where is the Green Sheep?* by Mem Fox & Judy Horacek

• *Where's Wally? Where's Waldo?* by Martin Handford

Online: Try these Tar Heel Readers:

https://tarheelreader.org/2018/07/30/where-9/

https://tarheelreader.org/2016/05/19/where-is-the-dog-2/

https://tarheelreader.org/2015/12/03/where-is-santa/

Writing: Write a list of all the places *where* you would like to go (in the community, to take a vacation, to go out to eat, etc.). Write about *where* you went during school (the classes, a special school trip, where you find things you use or need in school, etc.). At home, write about *where* you go to have fun (beach, park, playground, etc) or *where* you find things in your home, yard or community.

Ideas: Play a guessing game, to guess *where* you got an object. Pull the object out of a box and model the word *where*—"Where do you find this?" or "Where did I get this?" For example, if it is a sea shell, "Where do you find this?" (the beach); a fork, "Where do I get this?" (the kitchen); a pig, "Where is it from?" (a farm.), etc. Plan outings and model using the word "where." For example, "Where will we go? Where will we eat? Where will we shop? Where will we play? Where will we stop?." There are lots of "Seek/Look and Find" books where you need to search for objects in the picture. Model *where* as you look.

Art: *Flower or Leaf Prints!* Find some flowers or leaves that are mainly intact. Use different sizes and shapes as able. Place the flower or leaf between two sheets of paper, flatten them by carefully pressing down on top of the paper, then color over the top of it with a crayon or colored pencil. Watch as the shape of the flower or leaf appears on the top of the paper. You can add different colors, place different leaves or flowers together, or make small or large prints depending on the paper size. Prompt questions and comments with "where"" "Where did you find this/that?, Look where I am putting this!, Where is the _____?" etc.

Cooking: *Frozen Fruitcicles!* Make some fruitcicles from a favorite flavor of juice! Reduce the water by half when following the instructions on the can of frozen concentrate, then pour the juice in an ice cube tray (or little plastic cups if you would like them bigger), cover with plastic wrap, then carefully make a slice in the plastic above each cube/cup and place a popsicle stick inside. Freeze for two to four hours or more depending on size. If you want to make it "zippy," add Sprite or 7-Up instead of water to the concentrate. It may take a little longer to freeze, but it will add a little "zing" to the fruitcicle. Prompt: "Where is the _____?" (ingredient—juice, spoon, wrap, etc.). Have the students or your child take turns asking others "where" something is that follows next in the recipe.

LAMP WFL: Where (2 hits)—Question mark—Second row, 9th button; Third row, 12th button

Proloquo2Go (Crescendo Core) 77: Where—First row, 8th button

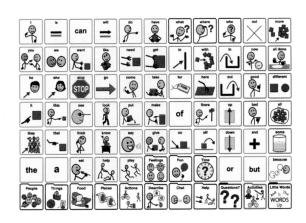

Sign: Where—Move index finger side to side with the wrist facing out (palm away from the face).

Core Word Guide: "You"

Phrases: You, You go, How are you?, Do you have _____?, What do you have?, Where are you?, How are you?, You have a _____, How do you feel?, You are _____, You have a _____.

Books/Literacy: The following books have repeated lines with the word "you":

• *Can You See What I See?* and other books by Walter Wick

• *Are You My Mother?,* by P.D. Eastman

• *What Do You Like?,* by Michael Grejniec

• *Mr. Brown Can Moo, Can You?* by Dr Seuss

• *Guess How Much I Love You,* by Sam McBratney

Online: Try these Tar Heel Readers:

https://tarheelreader.org/2018/03/17/you-5/

https://tarheelreader.org/2018/03/17/where-do-you-go-2/

https://tarheelreader.org/2018/03/17/you-are-2/

https://tarheelreader.org/2018/03/17/ask-a-friend/

Writing: Create phrases about a classroom friend or family member. "You are _____," "You can _____." Use "you" photos to write a class or family book in Pictello, or make a book with the "Tar Heel" reader. Write a card to a teacher, friend and/or family member. Emphasize phrases with "you"—you are nice, you help me, you are funny… See below in "art"—this gives an example of cards to make.

Games/Ideas: Go Fish "Do you have a _____?, What do you have?, You have a pair!, You have two!"

Art: *Make Note Cards!* Get some paper (plain, construction, wrapping paper) and cut a rectangle. Fold it in half and decorate the outside of your card. Use paints, markers, glue, glitter, cut-up wrapping paper, etc., to decorate. Look at some pictures of friends, classmates, teachers and/or family to help give choices of who to make/write the card to—you can do more than one person! On the inside of the card write a message. Start the card with the name of the person: "Dear _____, then sentences that start with "You." Remember to sign your name! Prompt: "You are _____ (nice, silly, pretty…), You make me feel _____, Thank you for _____, I like/love you," etc.

Cooking: *Make Scrambled Eggs!* Use two to four eggs, 2 Tbsp milk or 1 Tbsp water, & optional additions: cheese, dill, bacon pieces/bits, etc. Take turns breaking the eggs, one at a time, over a separate bowl (digging shells out will be easier). Put all the eggs together once the shells are gone, add the milk/water and any other ingredients. Whisk together then pour into a lightly greased/buttered pan or skillet. Lightly stir to scramble. Take turns adding ingredients and stirring: Prompt: "You go, You take a turn, You do, Do you want more?, Do you like it?" etc.

LAMP WFL: You—Pointing finger—First row, 4th button

Proloquo2Go (Crescendo Core) 77: You—Second row, 1st button

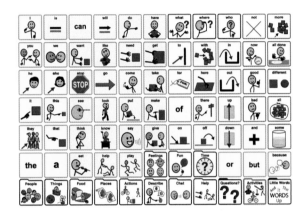

Sign: You—Point toward the person who is being referred to as "you."

Index

Core Word Art Activities

Note: the activities are located with the core word (in italics)

Bird Treats—*More*

Cinnamon Dough Ornaments—*Need*

Clear Spheres—*Not and Don't*

Crystal Balls—*That*

Flower or Leaf Prints—*Where*

Fruit Murals—*Like*

Gak—*Is*

Glue Art—*See*

Homemade Paint—*It*

Lake Michigan Wave Jars—*I*

Marble and Straw Painting—*Go*

Molding Clay—*Do*

Note Cards—*You*

Pasta Pictures, Sculptures or Jewelry—*Get*

People Drawing—*He and She*

Plant Flowers and Vegetables—*Put*

Pumpkin Carving—*Help*

Salad Spinner Art—*Mine*

Salty Ceramics—*Finished, All Done*

Sculpture Dough—*Have*

Shiny Paint—*What*

Sorting—*In and Out*

Suncatchers—*Stop*

Vegetable Painting—*Want*

Core Word Cooking Activities

Note: the activities are located with the core word (in italics)

Animal Biscuits—*Have*

Banana Shake—*I*

Boy and Girl Cookies—*He and She*

Brownies—*Put*

Butter Cookies—*Need*

Caramel Apple Fondue—*It*

Caramel Popcorn—*More*

Cheese Quesadillas—*Mine*

Cookie recipe with Decorations—*Go*

Dog Bone Biscuits (for dogs)—*Not, Don't*

Frozen Fruitcicles—*Where*

Fruit Salad—*Like*

Homemade Granola—*That*

Lemonade—*In and Out*

Milkshake—*Stop*

Pancakes (blueberry optional)—*Do*

Paradise Punch—*Finished, All Done*

Pasta Dishes—*Get*

Pizza—*Is*

Puppy Chow—*What*

Scrambled Eggs—*You*

Sugar Cookies—*See*

Toasted Pumpkin Seeds—*Help*

Vegetables and Dip—*Want*

Core Word Games

Note: the activities are located or can be used with the core word (in italics)

Bingo—*I, Have, It, What, You, Do*

Bubbles—*More, big, Little, Fast, Slow, Like, Don't/Do Not*

Connect Four—*In, Out, It, Is, Put, My, Turn*

Duck Duck Goose—*Go, You*

Freeze/Stop!—*Stop, Go*

Go Fish—*Do, You, Have, I, A, The, What*

Hi Ho Cheery-O—*Have, Do, You, What*

I Spy—*See, I, It, A, The, What, Do, You*

Memory—*It, Is, The You, Go, Have, Want, What, Do, I*

Mr. Potato Head—*I, Want, Do, You, Have, He, She, Put, It*

Music Games (where music stops and kids stop dancing): *Go, Stop, More, On, Off*

Play-Doh—*More, On, I, Want*

Puzzles—*On, Off, It, Here, Put*

Spot It—*See, It, I, Do, You, Is*

Swinging—*More, Stop, Up, Down, Go, Fast, Slow, Like, Don't/Do Not*

Uno—*My, Turn, I, Go, You*

Zingo—*I, Have, It, What, You, Do, Is*

Appendix 1

Reasons to Communicate

Note: This list includes different reasons to communicate, however, it is not extensive. (Adapted from Gail Van Tatenhove, Extreme Makeover Conference)

Gain Attention—help, help me, I need help, hello

Greet—hello, hi, see you, good bye, bye, later

Reject—no, not, I don't/do not want, I don't/do not like, not here, stop, no more, all done, finished

Request Object—I want it, want, I need that, Can I have?, Do you have?

Request Assistance—I need help, help, help me

Request Information/Ask Questions—what, where, why, how, who, when

Respond to Questions—yes, no, It is a _____, (labeling items or naming events)

Comment/Describe—It is _____, I ate a _____, It is _____ and _____, I see a _____, The dog is _____, He/She is_____, I don't/do not like it, I like it, It was _____.

Use Directives—go, stop, help

Use Associative Words/Location—big, little, red, hot, silly, up, in, on, out

Use Action Words—go, run, stop, swing, sleep, drink, get, eat, put

Complete Cessation—stop, no, all done, done, finished, end

Express Self and Others—mine, you, I, she, he, they...

Appendix 2

Core Word Phrases

Note: This list includes additional core words and phrases for communicative purposes.

A: I want a _____, It is a _____, That is a _____, Is it a ___?

All: It is all there, I want it all, It is all done

All Done: I am all done, Are you all done?

Am: I am sleepy, I am going to the _____, I am _____ (feeling: happy, sad, mad…), I am finished

An: It is an _____, I want an _____, They have an _____

And: You and me, I want _____ and _____, In and out, Am I done/finished?

Are: Are you there? We are going to _____, They are eating _____, Where are you?

Bad: It is bad, That is/was bad, It looks bad, Is it bad?

Big: It is big, That is big, I want a big _____

Can: Can I do it?, Can I have it?, I can do it, I can _____

Color: What color is it?, I like the color _____, What color do you want?, Do you like that color?

Come: Come get it, Come here (please), I want to come, Do you want to come?

Do: Do you have (a) _____?, I want to do it, Do you want more?, Do you need a _____?

Don't: Don't, I don't like it, I don't have it, Don't you want it?, Don't do that/it

Down: Go down, Put it down, Sit down

Drink: I want a drink, I want to drink more, Do you want a drink?, I want to drink _____

Eat: I like/want to eat _____, I don't like to eat _____, What do you (want to) eat?, Time to eat

End: The end, That/it is the end, Do you want to end it?, Go to the end

Fast: It is fast, That was fast, You were fast, Do you want to go fast?

Feel: I feel _____, What do you feel?, Do you feel _____?

Find: Help me find it, What did you find?, I need to find my _____

Finished: I am finished, He/she/they finished, I finished it.

Follow: Follow me, Do I follow you?, Do you want to follow me?

Get: I need to get more, Go get it/more, I want to get a _____

Give: Give it to me, What will you give?, Give it, I gave a _____

Go: I want to go to _____, I want to go, Do you want to go?, Let's go

Good: It is good, That is/was good, It looks good, Is it good?

Have: I have it, Do you have _____?, What do you have?, I have to _____

He: He is _____, He wants help, What is he doing?, He likes it, Where is he?

Hear: I hear it, Do you hear it?, What do you hear?

Help: Help me (please), Do you want help?, I need more help

Here: Put it here, Here it is, Can I put it here?, Here or there?

I: I want it, I am _____ (slow, big, hungry, happy), I like _____

In: Put it in, It is in, Go in, Is it in?

Is: It is mine, It is yours, Is it good?, It is _____ (good, bad, color word), It is a _____ (name of something), Is it mine/yours?, What/where is it?

It: It is good/bad, Do you have it?, I want it, I do not want it, What is it?

Know: I know that/it, Do you know it?, I don't know (it), What do you know?

Like: I like it, I do not like it, I like to eat _____, I/ you/he/she they like(s) _____, Do you like it?

Little: It is little, I want a little, A little more, Is it little?

Live: I live in a _____, Where do you live?, He lives in _____ (place: town, state).

Look: Look up/down, It looks good, It looks like (a) _____.

Love: I love you, I love you Mom/Dad/person, Do you love me?

Make: I want to make _____, Do you want to make _____?, I made a _____

Me: Get me some, Talk to me, Follow me, Help me, Can you help me?

Mine: That is mine, It is mine, Is it mine?

More: I want more (please), Do you want more?, There is more _____

My: My turn, That/it is my _____, Is it my turn?

Need: I need a/to _____, What do you need?, Do you need more?

New: I want a new _____, That is new, Do you want a new _____?

No: No, No I do not want it, No more, No thanks

Not: Do not do it, I do not like it, I do not want it, It is not mine

Now: Now, Not now, Now or later?, Do it now?, Can I go now?

Off: Turn off, Turn it off, It is not off, I like it off, I want it off

On: Put it on, On or off, Turn it on

Or: More or less?, This or that?, We can do _____ or do _____, Do you want _____ or _____?

Out: Go out, It is out, Put it out, Get it out, Is it out?

Play: I want to play, I want to play _____, Do you want to play?

Please: Please help me, I want more please, Please come here

Put: Put it there, Put it down/up, Put it in, Where did you put it?

Read: I want to read, It is time to read, Do you want to read more?, Read it to me

Ride: I want to ride it, Do you want a ride?, I like to ride a _____

Right: It is right, Go right, That is right, Is it right?, Am I right?

Said: He said _____, What was said?, I said to _____, He said what?

See: I see it, Do you see it?, What do you see?, I see a _____

She: She is _____ (descriptive word), She likes it, Does she like it?, She wants to _____.

Sit: Sit down, Time to sit, Do you want to sit?, Where do I sit?

Sleep: I need/want to sleep, Do you want to sleep?, It is time to sleep

Slow: It is slow, Do you want to go slow?, Go slow

Some: I want some, Go get some, He/she/they want(s) some, Do you want some?

Stop: Stop it, We need to stop, I want to stop, Do you want to stop?

Talk: My turn to talk, I want to talk, Do you want to talk?, Talk to me

That: That is good/bad, That is mine, I want that

The: I like/want the _____, The end, The _____ is mine

There: There it is, There they are, That/this goes there, Is it there?

They: They feel _____, They go to _____, They are going to _____, Do they want more?

Think: I think it is _____ (good, bad, slow, sad..), I want to think more, What do you think?

Time: It is time to go, What time is it?, Do I/we have more time?

To: Go to the _____, I want to see it, I like to _____, Do you want to _____?

Turn: My turn, Your turn, It is your/my turn, Do you want a turn?, I want a turn, Is it my/your turn?

Up: Go up, I want up, Look up

Want: I want it/_____, Do you want more?, What do you want?, I want to eat/go _____.

Was: It was _____ (descriptive word: fun, sad, red, big…), She/he was _____, Was it good?, What was it?

Watch: I want to watch _____, Do you watch _____?, Do you want to watch more?, What do you want to watch?

We: We want more, We go to _____, What do we want to do?, What do we do?

Wear: I wear _____, Wear it, I am wearing (a)_____, What do I wear?

Were: They were going to _____, Who were they?, Were you there?

What: What is it?, What do you want?, What is that?

Where: Where are we going?, Where am I?, Where is it?

Who: Who is it?, Who are you?, Who is that?, Who?

Will: Will you/I go?, What will I/we do?, What will I/we see?, Will it be hard/easy?

Work: I need to work, Do you work?, They are working

Yes: Yes, Yes I (do) want it, I said yes

You: Me and you, What do you want?, Do you have (a) _____?

Acknowledgments

The process it took to create this program was something that I could not have accomplished on my own. It included work and experience with many different people throughout my career. I would like to thank the students, families, therapists, and teachers that I have been able to work with who have brought invaluable insight and have motivated me to want to share what I have learned.

I would like to thank Amy Donaldson, who initially introduced core words and Prentke Romich Company's LAMP Words for Life program to me. Additionally, I want to recognize the many teachers, staff, parents, and students at Grand Haven Area Public Schools, Grand Haven, MI, who were all very supportive with learning about core words and trialing this program.

I owe Muskegon Area ISD at the Wesley School a special thank you. Particularly helpful to me was Mary Purtee and her incredible team of teachers and therapists. They graciously let me tour their program, shared resources and ideas for core words, and demonstrated ways to integrate them daily into the school curriculum.

I would like to thank Michele Staal, a parent who helped me to develop ideas for a practical home program using core words. This eventually led me to the "aha" moment of developing a 'curriculum' that coordinates school and home together with core words, while emphasizing AAC and verbal communication.

I would like to acknowledge AssistiveWare's Martijn Leopold, Prentke Romich Company's Michigan Representative Tina Pagnucco, William Vicars, Ed.D. of Lifeprint.com, and the Tar Heel Reader program from the University of North Carolina Chapel Hill for all of their support, guidance and permission to allow their program ideas and materials to be used throughout this text.

Thank you to Sherry Mitchell, Linda Bengston, and Donald Messinger, who generously offered their time and guidance with helping to publish this program. I also want to thank Tricia McDonald who led me to The Book Couple and ultimately to publication.

To Nancy Fortuna, thank you for graciously helping to edit the final version of this program. Your eye for detail and suggestions for clarity were much appreciated!

A special thank you goes to Miss Shannon Conners for her talents with modeling the ASL signs on the Core Word Guides. Also, thank you to her sister Emma, who helped to "manage" the photo sessions, and to their parents, who gave their enthusiastic support and permission.

Thank you to the lovely siblings on the cover photo, Layla, Magnolia, and Crosby. Your speedy assistance was much appreciated! I would like to include an additional mention to Ben for his enthusiasm.

I could not have published this without the expertise of Gary Rosenberg of The Book Couple. Thank you, Gary, for your patience, advice, and help with my entry into the very detailed world of publishing.

I would like to give a heartfelt thank you to my director, Kate Augustyn, Director of Special Education at Grand Haven Area Public Schools. She encouraged me as I developed the concept of this book and moved through the process of writing and publishing. Her enthusiasm and ongoing support allowed me to continue, especially when my confidence waned.

My parents and family were continuously there to listen, edit, and help share ideas with encouragement. Thank You!

Finally, I could not have written this program without the unending support of my wonderful husband, Neil, to whom I owe so much. Your patience, advice, edits, and continual encouragement have meant so much.

bad	there	end	stop	help	put	sleep
off	+s	the	fast	color	ride	turn
out	a	an	more	big	follow	watch
down	what	word / SPELL/NU	read	get	love	drink
no	in	to	feel	go	live	need
some	and	on	have	do	said	make
good	that	was	work	time	right	find
yes	please	were	like	come	think	eat
up	am	is	play	all	hear	sit
little	wear	are	new	want	slow	talk
mine	my	we	they	he	look	not
finished	me	I	you	it	she	CLEAR

word

+er +est

PREVERB

1 2 3

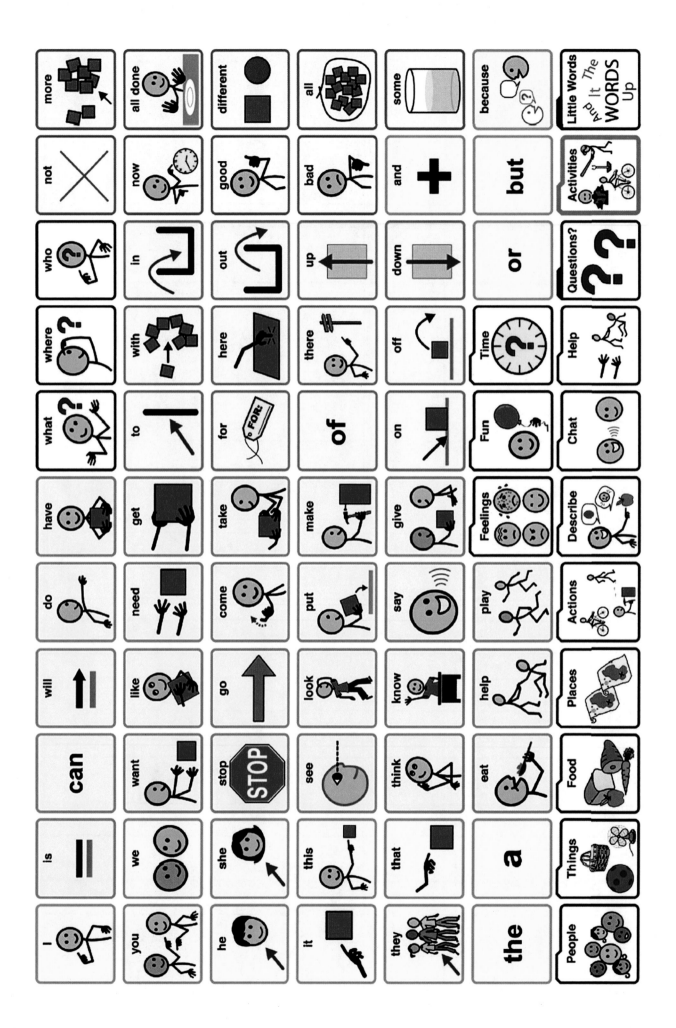

References

American Speech-Language-Hearing Association (ASHA). Web site information: ASHA.org.

AssistiveWare 2017, www.assistiveware.com, Proloquo@GO is a trademark of AssistiveWare. AssistiveWare as a learning organization, is made possible by the European Social Fund.

Baker, B., Hill, K., & Devylder, R. (2000). *Core Vocabulary Is the Same Across Environments.* Paper presented at a meeting of the Technology and Persons with Disabilities Conference at California State University, Northridge. http://www.csun.edu/cod/conf/2000/proceedings/0259Baker.htm.

Cross, R.T., Baker, B.R., Klotz, L.S. and Badman, A.L. (1997). Static and Dynamic Keyboards: Semantic Compaction in Both Worlds. Proceedings of the 18th Annual Southeast Augmentative Communication Conference, 9-17. Birmingham: SEAC Publications.

Hatch, P., Geist, L., Erickson, K., Greer, C., and Erwin-Davidson, L. *Using Core Vocabulary in Emergent Literacy Instructional Routines.* Handout at the 2017 ATIA Conference.

MacDonald, James D., (1989). *Becoming Partners with Children: From Play to Conversation.* Special Press. Web site information: www.jamesdmacdonald.org.

Picture Exchange Communication System (PECS)—Pyramid Educational Consultants, Developed by Andy Bondy, PhD and Lori Frost, MS, CCC-SLP, 1985

Prentke Romich Company (PRC). Web site information: www.prentrom.com Both the AAC Language Lab and The Center for Autism and Autism are affiliated with PRC.

Stubbs, M. (1986) Language development, lexical competence and nuclear vocabulary. In Durkin, K. (Ed.) *Language Development in the School Years.* London: Croom Helm.

Van Tatenhove, Gail M., PA, MS, CCC-SLP. *Core Vocabulary with Emergent & Context-Dependent Communicators in Special Education Classrooms.* Workshop presented in Muskegon, MI in May 2016.

Van Tatenhove, Gail M., PA, MS, CCC-SLP. *Extreme Make-Over: The AAC Edition*—Conference information. www.vantatenhove.com.

William Vicars Ed.D. Web site information: www.lifeprint.com (ASL University, 1997). ASL—American Sign Language.

About the Author

Jennifer Jacobs, MA, CCC-SLP, is a speech-language pathologist who is a graduate of The Ohio State University, where she received a Masters of Arts in Speech and Hearing Science. She has worked for nearly thirty years with both children and adults who have severe communication deficits, as well as with their families and other care providers. While living in Ohio, Jennifer was employed at the Ohio State University Medical Center, where she provided services for AAC (Augmentative Alternative Communication) as well as other traditional speech therapy services.

Her career began in Tuscany, Italy, where she worked privately for an American family and their child with special needs. While working at the Columbus Speech and Hearing Center, she co-authored a parent-child communication program for preverbal and early verbal children entitled "TALK." Throughout her professional life she has worked in a variety of settings, including clinical outpatient, acute rehabilitation, inpatient rehabilitation, as well as in classroom and home settings.

Jennifer currently works at Grand Haven Area Public Schools in Grand Haven, Michigan. She lives with her husband in Spring Lake, Michigan.

Made in the USA
Columbia, SC
30 July 2022

64350861R00051